The Business Design Cube

The Business Design Cube

Converging Markets, Society, and
Customer Values to Grow Firms
Competitive in Business

Rajagopal

BEP
BUSINESS EXPERT PRESS
Leader in applied, concise business books

First published in 2021 by
Business Expert Press, LLC
222 East 46th Street, New York, NY 10017
www.businessexpertpress.com

ISBN-13: 978-1-63742-016-4 (paperback)
ISBN-13: 978-1-63742-017-1 (e-book)

Business Expert Press Marketing Collection

Collection ISSN: 2169-3978 (print)
Collection ISSN: 2169-3986 (electronic)

First edition: 2021

10 9 8 7 6 5 4 3 2 1

With love to Arati

Description

This book discusses the three facets of the design-cube identified as design-to-market, design-to-society, and design-to-value through theoretical foundations, design arguments, managerial analysis, and best practices of companies. The design-to-market concept has been critically examined for customer-centric companies with focus on the current trend of coevolution and crowdsourcing approaches that drives the companies to practice critical thinking.

Keywords

design-to-market; design-to-society; design-to-value; business modeling; market competition; marketing strategy; socialization; co-creation; and coevolution

Contents

Preface

Businesses are growing selectively across industries and destinations despite most companies addressing the customer needs amidst the rising complexities of competition in the market. Darwinism can be well explained in the global business scenario as multinational companies are exploring remote markets while the hatched niche markets are seeking a way out to wider congregations. In this business dynamics, success is not guaranteed to the companies irrespective of their size, resources, and power. Reviewing several attributes of business today, a few questions often arise like why businesses fail, and, does design matter. SMART (strategic, measurable, accessible, responsive, and trustworthy), connected business designs raise a broad set of new strategic choices converging the attributes of markets, social responsiveness, and customer values to help companies perform as a corporate citizen. Creating social and customer values and securing competitive advantage by acquiring new capabilities to reshape industries have been the growing challenges for companies in emerging markets.

In large organizations, design perspectives are becoming central to the process of business modeling and strategy implementation. The concept of business design has emerged over time as a collective approach in an organization involving customers, stakeholders, and key functional partners. Most organizations have realized today that staying in business as learning organizations helps them grow competitively and consistently in the marketplace. Such business maxim has been described as "systems thinking" that leads to the design principle in business, known as "design thinking." Companies pursue this concept as a response to the mounting complexities in business operations. Design thinking in business has been conceived as an essential tool for simplifying the business operation by interlinking organization, society, and stakeholders, and more comprehensively humanizing the business. The extended principles of design thinking in business converge with the market attributes (market players, ethics, and business growth), social responsiveness (marketing with purpose), and customers' (stakeholders') value propositions. Such integrated, interlinked, and interlocked business philosophy guides the new business architecture as the "Design Cube." A design-centric business grows socially involving stakeholders, and evolves by inculcating high value among customers. The design cube advocates the cooperative philosophy as a win-win business model to manage the competitors and lead the market.

Market trends and consumer behavior are continuously changing, and social media is playing a critical role in determining marketing decisions. Volatility of consumer markets can have significant negative effects on risk-averse market share, profitability, and brand equity of the companies. However, volatility is one of the most important concepts in the competitive growth theory. The argument central to the theory of change management is that the companies operating in a competitive business environment consider consumer preferences, innovation, technology, and growth-related investments. Customer-centric companies, therefore, tend to build simpler products to help consumers choose the right product. In the design cube, companies that opt to stay customer-centric in business develop product design characterized by the emotional appeal of customers, and mend the market competition in their favor to improve performance. The best practicing companies develop emotional connections with the stakeholders through value-based design. Consumers exhibit positive behavior for products and services that ensure social pricing. Social interactions often motivate a sustainable and social consumption of products. The interplay of consumers within the social (inter-personal) and digital (remote response) platforms also helps companies go social and stay distinctive in the competitive marketplace. Consumers today are increasingly looking for brands that have a social purpose above functional benefit. As a result, most companies are taking social stands in highly visible ways. An effective, convergent business strategy creates social and customer values by coevolving the brand in the society. The connecting thread between society and business consists in developing cognitive ergonomics among the stakeholders and stimulating co-creation of business design. It is argued in the book that the socio-business convergence can be better understood through continuous learning about the consumer behavior.

Value is often measured in either economic or social terms. The blended-value proposition emphasizes that true value, which is a blend of economic, social, and environmental components, is indivisible. After the success of networking practices of business activities with social media over decades, profit-seeking firms have laid explicit emphasis on the creation of social value. This business philosophy has grown in nonprofit organizations as well. Social value is dynamic, and customer-centric companies continuously monitor the perpetual changes in social values, culture, and ethnicity. Consequently, companies have developed social corporate entrepreneurship, which intends to create social as well as financial value. The social business value is therefore defined as a function of corporate social initiatives to support business and the extent of social values absorbed in the society and the market. In order to drive the business deep into the social environment, companies adapt to the triadic philosophy of gaining social insights, ideation on blending business values in the society, and co-creating innovative socio-business strategies. The best practices reveal that these elements boost business results by driving business social and solving complex.

Successful companies like Nestlé, Whole Foods, and Apple bring business and society back together by creating shared value and generating economic value. Thus, companies deliver value for society by addressing its challenges. The social and value-oriented business designs tend to reconceive products and markets based on the social needs redefine productivity in the value chain and build social innovation clusters at their business hubs. Social collaborations focus on improving both business processes and performance. Social orientation of a business starts from a niche, links corporate-interest to shared interest, encourages productive competition, co-creates values, and builds trust among customers.

Accordingly, this book discusses attributes of the design-cube in creating social and customer values, and enhancing business performance of customer-centric companies. The effects of the design cube on managerial decision-making process and business performance constitute the core discussion in this book. Coevolution and value creation have been explained as the people's business approach, which benefits the companies in the long term. This book argues various dimensions of design-to-market, design-to-society, and design-to-value, and suggests developing innovative business models with alternate thinking to build

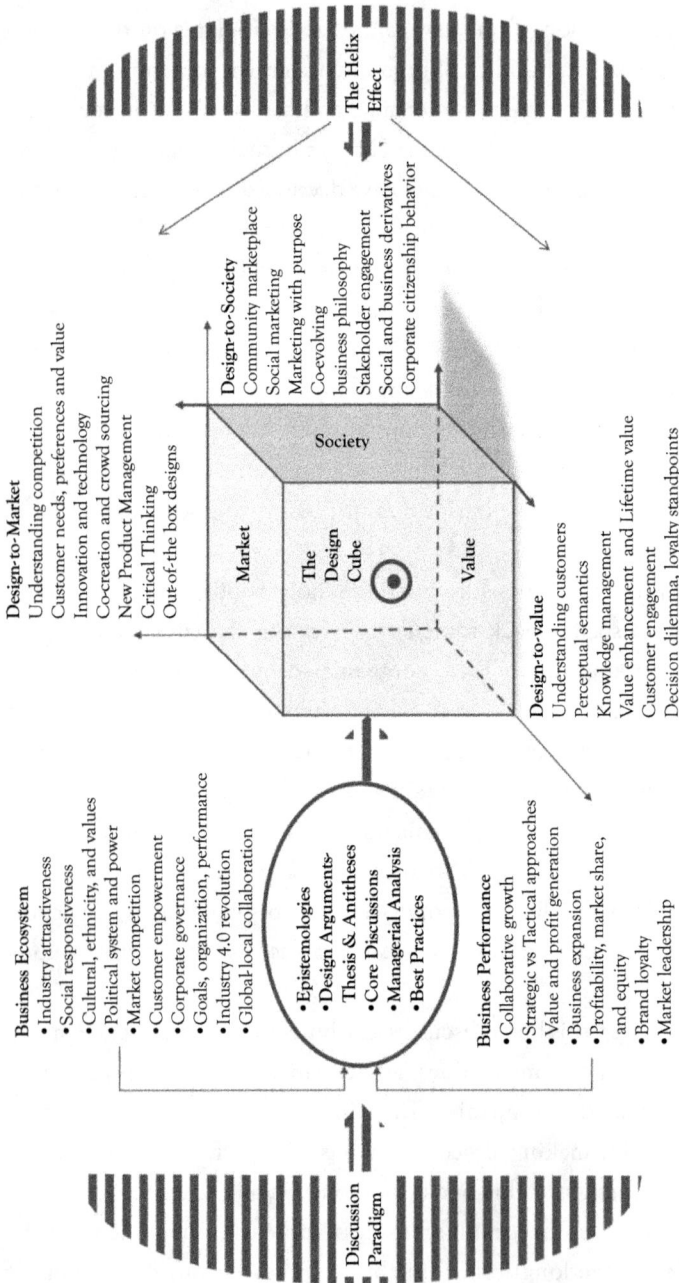

Design-to-Market
Understanding competition
Customer needs, preferences and value
Innovation and technology
Cocreation and crowd sourcing
New Product Management
Critical Thinking
Out-of-the box designs

Design-to-Society
Community marketplace
Social marketing
Marketing with purpose
Co-evolving business philosophy
Stakeholder engagement
Social and business derivatives
Corporate citizenship behavior

Design-to-value
Understanding customers
Perceptual semantics
Knowledge management
Value enhancement and Lifetime value
Customer engagement
Decision dilemma, loyalty standpoints

Society

Market

The Design Cube

Value

The Helix Effect

Business Ecosystem
• Industry attractiveness
• Social responsiveness
• Cultural, ethnicity, and values
• Political system and power
• Market competition
• Customer empowerment
• Corporate governance
• Goals, organization, performance
• Industry 4.0 revolution
• Global local collaboration

• Epistemologies
• **Design Arguments-
  Thesis & Antitheses**
• Core Discussions
• **Managerial Analysis**
• **Best Practices**

Business Performance
• Collaborative growth
• Strategic vs Tactical approaches
• Value and profit generation
• Business expansion
• Profitability, market share, and equity
• Brand loyalty
• Market leadership

Discussion Paradigm

Figure P.1 Discussion paradigm of the book

Source: Author

market competitiveness. The discussion model of the book is depicted in Figure P.1.

This book discusses the three facets of the design cube identified as design-to-market, design-to-society, and design-to-value through theoretical foundations, design arguments, managerial analysis, and best practices of companies, as illustrated in Figure P.1. The concept on design-to-market are discussed in the book in the context of innovation, technology, and new product development that help companies lead in the market competition. The design-to-market concept has been critically examined for customer-centric companies with focus on the current trend of coevolution and crowdsourcing approaches that drives the companies to practice critical thinking in business. Developing "out of the box" business designs in view of understanding market competition, consumer needs, preferences, and values have been discussed in the book.

Some management thinkers including C. K. Prahalad, Gary Hamel, Gerald Zaltman, Vijay Govidarajan, and Henry Mintzberg advocate that society is an integrated part of business, and companies should understand the social values embedded in the business. Therefore, most multinational companies like, Nestlé, Apple, and IBM develop their business models as "design-to-society" to not only create social value to their business but also to gain customer confidence as a principal tool to pave the path in the dense market competition today. Explaining this concept, the book discusses the reasons behind the companies in specific industries such as telecommunication (mobile phones), diet and health products (organic food), and transport (hybrid passenger automobiles), architecting community marketplaces, and developing social marketing strategies. The emerging concepts of "marketing with purpose" and coevolution of business designs are dealt as the core themes to illustrate "design-to-society" concepts that are being practiced sporadically by the large companies.

The last facet of the design-cube deals with the concepts and approaches of co-creating customer value, which is often at the dark side of the business plan. Understanding customers and developing their cognitive ergonomics are at the core of "design-to-value" concept discussed in this book. One of the pertinent questions on how knowledge management through corporate and social platforms helps in enhancement of lifetime value of customers has been addressed linking the customer engagement and corporate citizenship behavior. In addition, various elements of business ecosystem and business performance have been discussed in the book to support the contextual arguments laid on the three facets of the "design-cube."

This book examines the effects of socialization of corporate business and co-creating customer value. Reviewing a wide range of literature from statistical research studies to psychosocial implications of business strategies over time, discussions in the book analyze the emerging theory of corporate social responsibility, theory of social innovation, and theory of value co-creation. The concepts and models developed in the book are central to innovation, social responsive behavior of companies, and coevolution of business with customer. Thematically, the discussion on these theses are interpreted in terms of current consumer marketing and multibrand management issues of companies across market destinations. The focus of the discussion is precisely on penetration of innovation through social networks as an autocatalytic process that generates multiple market niches. The book deliberates upon the factors critical to the success of firms, which include diversity and cross-functionality. It is argued in the book that timely deployment of streamlined marketing strategies in chaotic markets could reduce the effects of social innovation, value spread among consumers, and growing complexities in the global and regional markets.

In a simplistic view, design-to-market can be explained through a 3Ds model comprising discover, design, and deliver. Most companies have been successful in finding growth by acquiring new companies and tapping new markets to manage products, segments, and destinations. Coevolution is the concept fundamental to the design cube. Customers offer solutions in the form of products or services. Companies then deliver these tangibles, and customers just do not buy. Consumer-centered market design delivers value and gain lead in the competition. Most companies have exhibited best practices in many industries, particularly those characterized by utilitarian products that hold emotional appeal. The social investment and co-creation of values lead to improved performance with product innovation. The short lifecycle of products is often affected by the creative disruption and the changing social values and lifestyle.

This book illustrates the causes and effects of helix effects in implementing the design cube-based business models across the markets of different size. Companies need to understand how to gain an inner analytic edge to defend value-driven business and augment the market share. Though companies draw some competition-based decisions through performance dashboards, the book suggests logical framework analysis and consumer-centered strategies for making sustainable decisions against uncertainties and the risk of deterioration in value-based performance. This book specifically discusses the following attributes of the design-cube in building effective business models:

- Linking business with society to enhance the performance of value-profit matrix
- Fitting business into value-based model to increase social foundation of business and create anthropomorphic effects among customers
- Staying ahead as the first movers, and reaping competitive advantage by bridging "value-defensive" business strategies, and
- Understanding cognitive ergonomics of consumers to regulate their drifts across brands, and streamlining loyalty through the theory of optimal distinctiveness and value creation.

Though value is an intangible concept, it is often viewed in either business or social terms. The "blended value proposition," as described in the design-cube and helix concepts in the book, asserts that business models reap strategic benefits when the indivisible value blends with stakeholder, social, and market-oriented components. This perspective is reexamined in this book in the context of for-profit and nonprofit organizations in the value creation process. Through multidisciplinary discussions, this book connects managers to dynamic markets and to behavioral domains of all entities playing role in the marketplace and offers strategic direction in making marketing decisions.

This book is divided into five chapters and accommodated in to three distinctive sections comprising the fundamental thinking, the design cube, and near and far effects. Chapter 1 discusses the concept of design cube in the context of design-to-market, design-to-society, and design-to-value business philosophies. Discussions on various aspects of the changing business ecosystem, value system in society and market, and transformation in the business processes are explained in the chapter with focus on contributions of the design cube on the business modeling process. Chapter 2 delineates the design-to-market strategy by explaining the attributes and ecosystem of marketing and design-thinking process with a view to gain competitive leverage and enhance business performance. The hybrid marketing mix comprising innovation and technology, and various hybrid management perspectives to optimize the effects of strategy design in marketing has been central to the discussions in this chapter. Chapter 3 discusses the conceptual and functional perspectives of social marketing and focuses on design-to-society approach by describing the interactive path, business and society convergence, policy implications, and society-driven growth. The effects of social networks and collective communication on business modeling in the context of user-generated content are also addressed in this chapter. The design-to-value philosophy is streamlined with the design-to-society and design-to-market concepts are discussed in Chapter 4. The strategy pyramid constituting the firm, society, and business has been discussed comprehensively in the context of design-to-value marketing modeling. The chapter also discusses behavioral determinants in the context of creating customer lifetime value. Chapter 5 discusses business modeling process in the context of value-driven indicators. The double and triple helix effects on business modeling have been discussed in the chapter in the context of growing design market, design-to-society, and design-to-value philosophies. In addition, this chapter deliberates upon the changing issues concerning market competition and value creation strategies.

This book bridges theory and applications of design elements in business by linking market competition, customer value, and society in managing multibrand and multimarket paradigms to achieve long-term business performance. A balanced business model with these triadic elements tends to reduce chaotic effects, decision imperfections, and negativity on consumer values. The book discusses dual, triple, and quadruple helix effects on business performance of companies by integrating competitive behavior of companies, social involvement, customer value, coevolution, and sustainability. Discussions on helix effect argue that companies need to consider a broader perspective to enhance the effectiveness of business models by implementing applied marketing decisions and putting the consumer first in the business management process.

I have been teaching consumer behavior, marketing strategy, and international business management courses in MBA programs for two decades, during which my knowledge, insights, and critical thought process have periodically updated. I found that the design thinking–based business modeling has not been discussed in any of these courses as no textbooks have identified it as a topic of interest. In reality, the design thinking has emerged as central to business modeling and strategy development process. I felt it necessary to share with students the applied concepts of design cube that affect the decisions at both levels of customers and companies. Therefore, this book is an outgrowth of the thought process from a classroom to a wider platform of audience. I have taught the aforementioned courses from the perspectives of delivering contemporary practices in marketing management to students, putting them through various real-life business scenarios. This helped them analyze the market complexities and gain confidence in developing the right business modeling and marketing strategies to do business in the competitive marketplace. Initially, I worked out a teaching agenda on strategic marketing and business expansion models for global companies and discussed them at length in the classroom, encouraging timeless discussions on the subject that helped in developing new conceptual frameworks on the subject. Some of my research papers on business modeling and customer-centric marketing in the emerging markets have been published in the international refereed journals that had driven new insights on the subject. Accordingly, filtered and refined concepts and management practices, endorsed with applied illustrations and updated review of literature on managing business in the overseas destinations, have been presented in the book.

This book is a good fit for managers to learn the intricacies of business modeling. It is also a notable learning resource for researchers, and students of marketing strategy, marketing research, business analytics, and courses in decision sciences. This book has been developed to serve as a managerial guide and think tank for the graduate students engaged in studying courses on business strategy, and marketing. Besides serving as a reference book to the students, this would also be an inspiring book for managers, market analysts, and business consultants engaged in decision-making process for developing marketing strategy. This book will contribute to the existing literature and deliver new concepts to the students and researchers to pursue the subject further. By reading this book, working managers may also realize how to converge best practices with corporate strategies in managing business at the destination markets while students would learn the new dimensions of marketing strategies.

Rajagopal
Mexico City
November 30, 2020

Acknowledgments

In completing this volume of the book, I have been benefited by the discussions of my colleagues within and outside the EGADE Business School. I am thankful to Dr. Osmar Hazael Zavaleta Vazquez, Associate Dean of Research at EGADE Business School, Mexico, who has been encouraging in my new endeavors. I thank all my students of graduate and doctoral programs at EGADE Business School for sharing enriching ideas on the subject during the classroom discussions, which helped in building this book on the framework of innovative ideas. This book is an outgrowth of my teaching new concepts in qualitative research to doctoral research scholars and working managers in the MBA program.

I also acknowledge the outstanding support of Robin J. Zwettler and Scott Isenberg, Executive Editors of Business Expert Press, who critically examined the proposal, guided the manuscript preparation, and took the publication process forward. My special thanks to Dr. Naresh Malhotra, Regents Professor Emeritus at Scheller College of Business, Georgia Tec University and series editor on consumer behavior subject at Business Expert Press, for his guidance and encouragement in bringing out this volume. I am thankful to various anonymous referees of my previous research works on innovation and technology management that helped me in looking deeper into the conceptual gaps and improving the quality with their valuable comments.

Though it was a solo journey with this publication project from ideation to manuscript preparation, I must acknowledge the encouragement from senior academics to proceed with the project. I express my deep gratitude to my wife Arati Rajagopal, who always reminded me of this task over other deadlines in the agenda. She also deserves kudos for copyediting the manuscript rigorously before submitting it to the publisher.

CHAPTER 1

The Concept Map

Overview

This chapter delineates the concept of design-cube comprising design-to-market, design-to-society, and design-to-value constituents. Discussions on various aspects of changing business ecosystem, value system in society and market, and transformation in the business processes explain the concept map of the design-cube and its applications in the business modeling. This chapter presents many corporate examples that are in line with the design-cube concepts. There is a discussion included on systems effects of systems thinking on business performance. This provides a new vision to understand embedded elements and their role also in transforming corporate philosophies from conventional wisdom to contemporary strategies to gain competitive leverage in the marketplace.

Business Ecosystem

Business today is founded on a triadic elements of market, society, and customer values. The core and contextual attributes in a business form the ecosystem of a business, which is a strategic perspective of managing business in a competitive marketplace. The notion of business ecosystem addresses the relative concepts of collaboration and competition, such as customer-centric and market-led strategies of business, in both predetermined and dynamic business systems. Broadly, the extrinsic attributes of a business ecosystem include innovation (social and market-based), a competition constituent (opportunity mapping, elements of oligopoly and monopsony, and market taxonomy), and social business philosophies of companies (Parente et al. 2018). Traditional firms considered macro elements in the business as exogenous drivers of business ecosystem and focused on controllable variables like organizational design, work culture, and marketing mix. The exogenous elements like competitors, suppliers, stakeholders, and business partners have become endogenous management factors of the business ecosystem. Technology plays a major role in the business ecosystem today, which has evolved from an internally focused factor to customer-facing attributes, leading to agile business development. The bilateral factors in the business ecosystem include government, business partners (manufacturing, logistics, and marketing), financial institutions, and information technology providers.

Many companies have developed integration capabilities to establish upstream and downstream alliances through technology platforms. In conventional firms, the integration points are often static. The dynamic business ecosystems allow bilateral connections with a small, preselected group of partners and large firms in production and business operations such as manufacturing, distribution, and marketing activities. Successful business ecosystems develop operational networks between intra-organizational (across functional divisions) workstations and market players. Companies with such functional networks are able to integrate required elements of business ecosystem. Nonetheless, new enterprises struggle to collaborate with the upstream market players and compete in these markets. Such efforts of new ventures demand strategic thinking to leverage a firm's resources and capabilities to establish strategic alliances. Strategic thinking helps new entrants adjust ecosystem with the socioeconomic, cultural, and market-led factors that influence one another and stimulate the management of the design-cube comprising design-to-market, design-to-society, and design-to-value. The business ecosystem is fundamentally based on these triadic design pillars. Large companies tend to explore radically new technology to disrupt existing markets, while the new entrants focus on pursuing value-adding improvement in the existing products and technologies on the frugal innovation platform. In this process of orchestrating business ecosystems, multinational companies and joint ventures follow an integrative and long-term perspectives in business embedding business goals and strategic interests in decision making. Such strategic business goals help these firms develop backward and forward linkages with suppliers and buyer-groups to develop operational integration (Zahra and Nambisan 2012).

In the competitive business environment, large firms operate with open ecosystems to gain competitive leverage by commercializing open-innovation and reverse-innovation products. This strategy helps firms in delivering high customer value and inculcate perceptions among customers on collective creativity. Consequently, firms can retain the loyalty and support of ecosystem partners and stakeholders to ensure their continued performance in the marketplace. Continuous learning and exploring ways to catch-up with changes in the industry drive firms to stay agile with the dynamic business ecosystems. Industrial marketing firms have moved today from relationship-management goals to ecosystems-orchestration process. Business environment today is hierarchically arrayed within industry with transitional multimodal business system across large firms. Large firms within industries (such as pharmaceuticals) develop business consortiums, and focus on collaborative strategizing, and expanding the key partners geographically. The changing business ecosystems today drive greater flexibility in strategic partnership by allowing firms to develop collaborations contextual to the collective intelligence, social values, and benefit-spread across the stakeholders (Reeves et al. 2015).

Most virtual business players like Amazon, Google, Alibaba, and Uber have adapted to technology-focused ecosystem as hubs within the networks of customers, suppliers, and producers. These hubs develop backward and forward functional linkages to support the core and peripheral functions to orchestrate the business ecosystem. However, a single or predetermined ecosystem does not support businesses of all firms due to variability in business attributes of each firm. For example, while Google has been a successful and profitable enterprise, Spotify and Uber are struggling continuously to make adjustment with the business ecosystem. But regardless of how successful they prove to be, they are adopting a different set of strategies than the traditional firms engaged in doing business under the contemporary business ecosystem (Birkinshaw 2019). Companies needs to understand the business ecosystems and exploit opportunities in the following ways:

- Identify a keystone contribution.
- Develop employee engagement, accountability, and internal consistency in managing revenue streams with global-local business partners.
- Explore the advantages of the ecosystem to innovate and renew the keystone contribution.

Keystone contribution of a firm is a distinguished activity or a process that provide unique business proposition to the firm and enable it to own and control its operations. Such keystones are considered as essential constituents of the business ecosystem to create value for customers. The unique product designs of original equipment manufacturers (OEM) in manufacturing telecommunication chips constitute keystone contributions. The ownership and control of chip makers restrict the mobile phone instrument manufacturers to switch to designs from an alternative supplier. The OEMs establish tollgates to control the flow of revenue through license fees, royalties, or commissions on transactions besides the quality checks on products within the ecosystem. Firms draw advantages from the ecosystems toward new and incremental innovations. The business ecosystems help firms in text mining, and analyze collective intelligence. Alibaba, Flipkart, and Amazon aggregate and analyze user data from multiple websites as a part of their decision-making ecosystem on shopping preferences and consumption patterns (Williamson and De Meyer 2019). Dynamic business ecosystems demonstrate customization against standardization (personal computers, 3D printers etc.), closed-loop decision processes, asset sharing (infrastructure, brand, supply chain network), collective knowledge pool, and collaborative ecosystem to optimize the business performance of the firm a collaborator. No specific business model of a firm has displayed all the aforementioned elements in the dynamic ecosystem, but having a higher number of dynamic attributes of business ecosystem usually correlates with a greater chance of success by business transformation (e.g., Kavadias et al. 2016).

In the changing business trends today, a firm is no longer an independent strategic actor; it is dependent on collaborations and strategic alliances. Its success depends on collaboration with stakeholders and market players, and strategic alliances with other firms in a multisectoral ecosystem. Such transformations in business ecosystems are focused on following the strategic decision attributes toward:

- Moving from market-oriented to customer-centric strategies with focus on creating value among collaborators. Such business strategy helps the collaborating firms take initiatives on customer-centric innovations,

- Determining the role of principal and collaborating firms in pursuing the design cube comprising design-to-market, design-to-society, and design-to-value perspectives in transforming business ecosystems
- Drafting the terms-of-reference of collaboration among the partnering firms, and providing the task or project governance options. The terms-of-reference would guide the accessibility of collaborative firms within the ecosystem and describe the exclusivity in roles,
- Developing appropriate inter- and intra-organizational scenarios to design approaches for cooperative competition (coopetition). The ability to collaborate with partners can shift according to the intrinsic and extrinsic factors embedded in the business ecosystem, and
- Managing multiple ecosystems based on the organizational capabilities, competencies, and market requirements.

Some orchestrators are able to manage multiple ecosystems successfully by covering different parts of the collaborative tasks leading to diverse business expansions. For example, General Electric (GE) has many channel partners and system integrators in various business divisions. Channel partners constitute the GE Digital ecosystem and play catalytic role in sales and value creation regardless of whether they act as an extension of the GE Digital sales team or distribute GE Digital products independently (Jacobides 2019).

Business ecosystems are becoming complex by developing pro-environment products for consumer and industrial use as firms are addressing global sustainability challenges including climate change, resource depletion, and ecosystem loss. Transformations caused due to the sustainability perspectives in business is being successfully managed by some companies through effective collaborations. Large firms are developing long-term value propositions to collaborate with business partners in new ways that treat fragile and complex ecosystems as a whole. For example, apparel coalition led by Nike, Patagonia, and Walmart describe new collaboration models that create shared value and address environmental protection across the value stream. However, the partnership ecosystem is not always favorable for the cross-country business expansions. The executives of Bharti Airtel, India's largest mobile services operator, during its business expansion in African countries, discovered some unwarranted challenges including cultural differences between their Indian and African employees, an infrastructure poorer than expected with higher-than-anticipated costs, a monopolistic distribution network, strong competitors, a weak partner ecosystem, and a market unresponsive to tariff cuts. These challenges have significantly disrupted the predetermined business ecosystem of the firm and its collaborators (Palepu and Bijlani 2012).

Incubation of innovations has emerged as a new model of startup facilitation in most developing economies. Venture capitalists review the incubators and assess the projected growth and profitability in businesses to invest. The venture capitalists review the incubators to diversify risky investment portfolios, while the prospecting entrepreneurs approach the incubators to review the economically viable and technologically feasible support for startup projects. Innovation incubators of the firms face challenges and opportunities to grow competitive in the marketplace. However, there exists the embedded investment and entrepreneurial risks. Broadly, there are five incubator archetypes such as the university incubator, the independent commercial incubator, the regional business incubator, the company-internal incubator, and the virtual incubator (Carayannis and von Zedtwitz 2005; Rajagopal 2020a). Strategies like enhancing the capability and competence; investment in internal research and development; and globalization through strategic alliances, and mergers and acquisitions push local enterprises toward helix effect. These enterprises not only succeed in local markets over time but can also build global value chains. New ventures can improve their business ecosystem to ensure effective business performance with the collaborators by reinforcing the following considerations (*e.g.* Kanter 2012):

- Converging knowledge pool (collective intelligence and entrepreneurial education) with organizational culture to create new venture, partnerships, and business goals
- Bridging creativity and marketing strategies to implement new ideas into market-ready enterprises

- Linking small and large enterprises to promote the growth of new entrants in the industry and develop strategic alliances with the large corporations though innovation enterprises
- Improving the match between entrepreneurial education and entrepreneurial opportunities
- Stimulating public policies to link knowledge-creativity-innovation and markets within an industry
- Developing transformational leadership across sectors to develop regional strategies and produce scalable business models.

It is often challenging for the small companies to adapt to a structural business model over the traditional family-based organizational structure. Such business confinement needs small firms in emerging markets to coevolve with large firms and catch-up with them to improve the manufacturing and marketing processes, and the productivity rather than engaging in frugal innovations for niche markets.

Shifts in Business Philosophy

Major structural shifts in the global economy are creating new opportunities in transaction banking, particularly in trade finance. International trade is growing faster than global GDP, and Asia is now the center of global expansion, driving trade growth in other emerging markets and in developed economies as well. The global economy faces significant challenges as it continues to integrate high levels of public debt in Europe and North America that is causing the fear of a negative impact on GDP growth. Companies intending to go global exhibit two apparent objectives: to take advantage of opportunities for growth and expansion, and survival in the business amidst growing competition. However, firms that fail to pursue global opportunities eventually lose their domestic markets and may be pushed aside by stronger and more competitive global firms. One of the revolutionary business dynamics at the grassroots has been the rapid mergers and acquisitions of family businesses with equal-size or larger firms within the industry. Such shifts among family firms have shown vertical or horizontal expansions. In addition, the intergenerational succession of firms also influences the expansion of family businesses through mergers and acquisitions. The effect of succession also develops transformational leadership in family business for survival and augmenting the performance in the competitive marketplace. In family enterprises, intra- and inter-company relationships form a vital source of social capital, and help firms in converging design-to-market and design-to-society business models to create organizational value. Social capital in family business firms contributes to developing enhanced socioeconomic goals, financial and human resources, and governance structures (Zellweger et al. 2019).

Innovation entrepreneurship is a convergence of startup enterprises and the sponsoring companies, which moves from the stage of initiation to the systematic project management, to commercialization, and finally develops sustainable innovation through incremental innovations. Companies need to invest substantial resources toward consumer education in order to create consumer demand. Besides, they also need to carry out product demonstrations such as "do-it-yourself" and adaptive customization by allowing consumers to use the new products for a reasonable period, and perceive the value for money associated with the products. However, the opportunities for open innovation, incremental innovation, and enhancement of the use value of innovative products over the stages of product lifecycle finally take the innovation business projects to the initiation stage of the next generation innovative products (Rajagopal 2019).

The emphasis on co-creating innovation and managing innovation business projects in partnership with the local companies is gradually generating technological breakthroughs, allowing emerging companies to reduce the time to bring innovative products and services to market. The recent trend of carrying out innovation in the business-to-consumer and business-to-business segments by companies involve different ways of deploying price and volume advantages in global competition. Large companies practice outsourcing of innovation, collaborating with startup enterprises, investing in open innovation, and engaging in driving public–private partnerships. For example, large companies from emerging markets such as Lenovo Group Ltd. (China), and Godrej Consumer Products (India); and Internet players such as Tencent Inc. (China) are pioneering new ways of industrializing the innovation. These companies are engaged in simultaneous engineering by leveraging quick launch, test, and improve cycles combining vertical hierarchy for effective control of manufacturing systems with horizontal flexibility. These companies allow autonomy among the innovation teams to steer the new insights and experiments within peer groups (Rajagopal 2016). Continuous growth in innovation and technologies is the principal stimulant for companies to gain competitive differentiation and leadership in the global markets, and gain high brand equity to drive consumers toward new buying preferences and exploring new market segments. However, it is often hard for consumers to adopt innovations, gain confidence in deriving values appropriately, and derive competitive advantages from the innovative offerings over the existing and predetermined products and services. Companies growing in a competitive marketplace monitor both new and incremental innovations to explore their influence on firms' survival and growth. In addition, the market orientation, firm's size, its international dimension, and age of the business leader at entry are the control variables most influential on survival (Ortiz-Villajos and Sotoca 2018).

Advancements in the information technology and various computer-aided business applications have drifted the conventional business philosophy of *marketing-to-customer* (objectivity in business models) to *marketing-with-customer* (collaborative business models). The latter shift in the business philosophy considers customers and market players as associates in business, and intends to co-create strategies and coevolve business in both vertical and horizontal dimensions. Such shift in the business philosophy has encouraged the role of collective intelligence in building customer-centric strategies and co-creating customer-centric innovations to develop standalone posture in the competitive marketplace (Miotti and Sachwald 2003). The growth of virtual commerce (electronic and mobile commerce) has emerged as the most popular outgrowth of marketing-with-customer philosophy. The virtual commerce has been further aided by the augmented reality to provide 3-D (dimension) perceptions and feel congruent with the brick-and-mortar buying experience. Augmented Reality (AR) is one of the interactive technologies that enhances consumer emotions and perceptions and develops cognitive ergonomics. AR influences anthropomorphic feelings of consumers and contributes to the retail anthropomorphism (Esch et al. 2019). Interactive technologies are enhancing the competitiveness of retailing firms by transforming traditional business models such as the offline menus of restaurants and travel packages. Artificial Intelligence technologies are widely used to support different AR experiences in retail operations. Retail firms have adopted chatbots to interact with consumers through various communication channels including social media, live chat, and SMS to complement the AR experience. In addition, digital networks support conversational commerce, which helps companies not only assist customer in product selection, but also support their choices throughout the shopping and decision-making processes (Leung and Yan-Chan 2020).

Transforming consumer experience from 2D marketing to 3D reality has empowered customers to adopt the new shopping philosophy of *knowing, believing,* and *doing* to make buying decisions on both brick-and-mortar and virtual platforms. Interactive online and mobile technologies enable consumers to get engaged in real time comparisons of attributes, prices, promotions, and augmented services of products and services. Such interactive technology stimulates the purchase intentions of consumers. Mobile interactive applications help smaller firms overcome the traditional retailing systems and drive through economies of scale to gain competitive advantages and improve bargaining power. Technology enables interactive relationships in retail settings to have both audio and visual effects of communication, and improves retailer–customer relationship. The functionality of interactive technology increases *scalability in business, precision* in managing target customers, and *mobility in horizontal expansion of business across geo-demographic segments* by enhancing the convenience of customer to buy products. Retailers draw emphasis on cost-effective technologies, which motivates customers to adapt to the technology to enjoy shopping excitingly (Liao and Shi 2009).

Rapid adaptation to the changing technologies in businesses has also made significant impact on the micro, small, and medium enterprises that has stimulated their transition from conventional manufacturing and business models to the digital entrepreneurship. Digital technologies have significantly contributed to the creativity and customer values in the new business ventures. The growing technologies are able to leverage the potential of interfirm collaborations and collective intelligence. The technological adaptation in businesses broadly supports the design-cube perspectives in the context of design-to-market, design-to-society, and design-to-value strategies. Customer-friendly technologies based on customer-centric business designs are able to launch more robust and sustainable entrepreneurial initiatives. The digital entrepreneurship ecosystem consists of following elements (e.g. Elia, et al. 2020):

- Digital actors (technology developers, providers, and entrepreneurs)
- Digital activities (computer-aided designing, manufacturing, and services)
- Digital motivations (market competition, public policies, growth initiatives)
- Digital organization (seamless operations, digital infrastructure self-service modules)
- Digital resources (transfer of technology, capital management, human resources, user interface)
- Digital operations (communication, monitoring, evaluations, networking)

Digital technologies enable entrepreneurial activities to gain competitive advantage and evolve in the market to manifest digital products or services, digital platforms, digital tools and infrastructure, digital artifacts, and Internet-enabled service innovations. Such digital business models engage with customers and stakeholders through online platforms by offering customized products and services catering to multivariate demands. Companies using digital technologies often integrate social media to acquire collective intelligence, outsource activities, and encourage customer engagement and social governance (Kuester et al. 2018).

Successful marketing of technology-based products depends on the attributes of technology; cost of consumer education on the technology advances; breakeven period of marketing technology; the associated government, societal, and industrial marketing linkages; and specialty institutions like pharmaceutical research, social innovation research, and consumer technology research. Marketability of technology is also driven by anticipated market share of technology products in the long term, and their contribution to the profit of marketing organizations. As the technology grows faster than its adaptability among consumers, there exists higher competition in the technology market. Therefore, branding of technology (like Intel computer processors), and achieving brand equity are complex phenomena. Strong alliance with global brands could help the companies on marketability of emerging technology. The diffusion of digital technologies has created diverse opportunities for the development of small and medium enterprises by leveraging collaboration with large firms and using collective intelligence through social media to develop customer-centric businesses. The convergence between entrepreneurship and digital technologies has been responsible for creating a new generation of entrepreneurs, who tend to use digital technologies and Internet extensively in various business processes (Giones and Brem 2017). Consumers demand clear market communication for technology products emphasizing the competitive advantage, and their effectiveness in business-to-business and business-to-consumers market segments. It is also important for marketers to know about lead value of the technology against the competing technology brands. Market entrepreneurship today has developed in regional markets because of the increasing global competition and is aimed at introducing novelty, innovation, or improvement into the production and technology exchange processes within the industry. Thus, the governments of developing countries stimulate productive entrepreneurship and make enterprises practical and operational through various public policies (Rajagopal 2019).

The Design Cube

Marketing today is not just a profit phenomenon for most successful global and multidomestic companies; it is rather a ensuring a sustained growth in marketplace by creating social and stakeholder values. Consequently, the business models are built around triadic constituents including market (competition), society (social needs, responsibility, and sustainability), and values (customers and stakeholders). These elements are integrated to explain the design cube through the design-to-market, design-to-society, and design-to-value perspectives in contemporary business modeling process. The major concern for large firms today is not to explore new markets, expand portfolios, and go global, but to tailor their business strategies to fit to social, ethnic, and consumer culture. Such strategic alignment determines the degree of standardization or adaptation appropriate to the society, stakeholders, and customers in creating Strategic business models. Firms converge the design cube elements to build the overall business strategy, determining which products and services benefit in the competitive, social, and consumption ecosystems. Accordingly, companies develop strengths to defy social and cultural barriers and analyze trade-offs to develop appropriate the marketing mix strategies (e.g. Quelch and Hoff 1986).

Unilever in Brazil has moved to the bottom-of-the-pyramid market segment to cater to the low-income consumers and create social value for its brands. The strategy of the company is a good-fit to the business design cube as the company tends to expand its market to the low-income consumer segment, and create values congruent with the society and consumers. Unilever has focused on diverting resources from its premium brands to target the lower-margin segment of low-income consumers, and reposition the existing brands to avoid launching a new brands or extensions of the existing brands. Brands at the bottom-of-the-pyramid targeted to deliver value to low-income consumers have emerged as social consumption products over time without cannibalizing premium brands of the companies (Guimaraes and Chandon 2004). Similarly, the *Shakti* (meaning power in Hindi language) project aimed at empowering women in marketing of products of Hindustan Unilever Limited (HUL) in India has made a strong social intervention to create value among customers at the bottom of the pyramid. Project *Shakti* enables rural women in villages across India in inculcating an entrepreneurial mindset and become financially independent marketer of HUL products. In an attempt to provide regular income, these women entrepreneurs are trained on basic principles of distribution management and familiarization with the company's products. In this process, rural sales promoters coach women by familiarizing them with HUL products in order to manage their businesses better. Imparting such training in women entrepreneurs develops soft skills of negotiation and communication, and prepares them as business associates of the company. This strategy of empowering rural women to expand the market horizon of HUL is consistent with the elements of the design cube.

The principal attributes of the design cube concept are the convergence of business strategies with market, society, and value perspectives. Firms following such triadic convergence are able to develop value-based business models and measure their performance with purpose. The engagement of firms with the design cube concept helps them in co-creation and coevolution with customers and stakeholders. The constituents of the triadic elements of the design cube along with the features of enablers of this concept are illustrated in Figure 1.1.

The increasing use of market research tools to understand the trends of market competition has helped firms conceptualize the design-to-market strategies. A large number of local firms in emerging markets could be able to manage a successful way out of market competition from multinational companies. These firms have built out-of-the-box strategies to manage product and services in the competitive markets by focusing on customer needs, preferences, and values. The design-to-market philosophy advocates co-creation and collective intelligence to develop innovation and technology-based products. Figure 1.1 illustrates that firms need to integrate all attributes discussed earlier by exercising critical thinking in implementing design-to-market concepts. The design-to-market concept is meticulously associated with the social and value perceptions generated by the firm. The design-to-society perspective is built around the broad philosophy of community marketplace and social marketing. Local firms customize products and services to meet customer needs in niche markets, and later go after economies of scope. This is a linear path from design-to-society to manage design-to-market strategies in a larger market area. Local firms develop business models by considering social derivatives in business to gain competitive advantage. The corporate social responsibilities and marketing with purpose (social, sustainability, and consumer welfare) inculcate the corporate citizenship behavior among firms of all sizes.

Business competition is a major concern of the firms that face irregular competition increase market share and maximize profits. While small and medium firms are vulnerable to market competition effects, large firms also are not immune from such effects. Competition among firms is commonly observable in the product marketing across the geo-demographic segments. The design-to-market strategies are developed congruent to

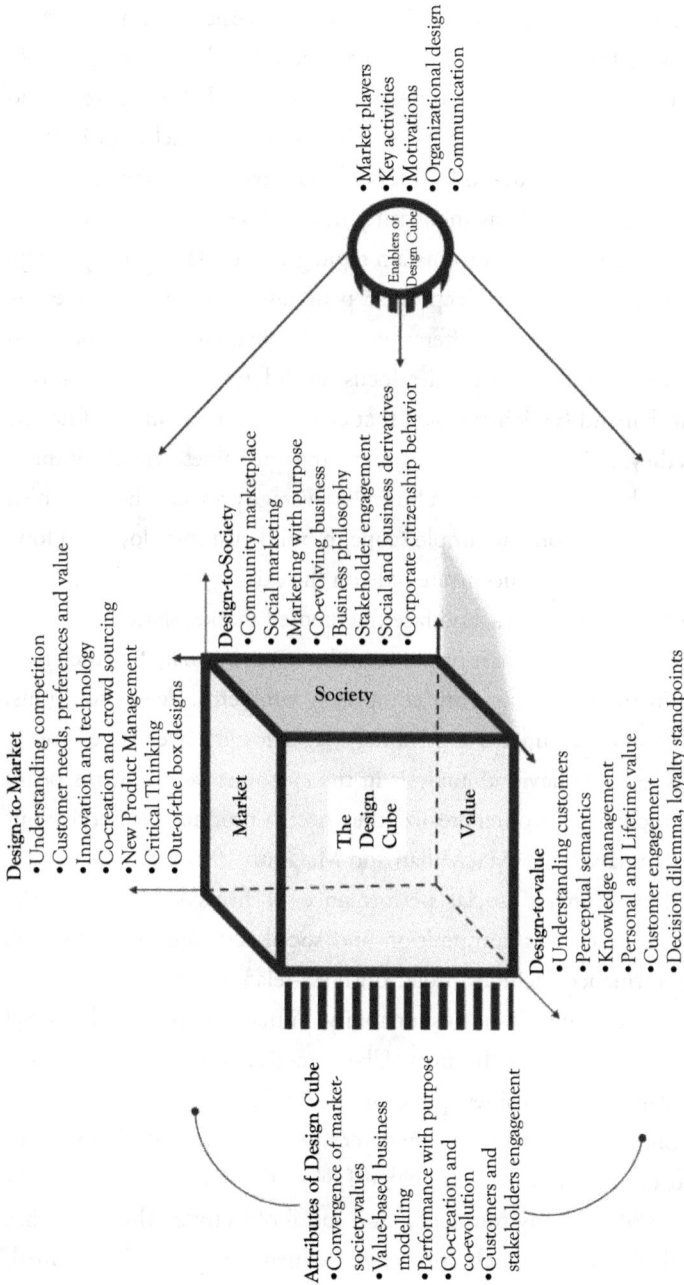

Design-to-Market
- Understanding competition
- Customer needs, preferences and value
- Innovation and technology
- Co-creation and crowd sourcing
- New Product Management
- Critical Thinking
- Out-of-the box designs

Design-to-Society
- Community marketplace
- Social marketing
- Marketing with purpose
- Co-evolving business
- Business philosophy
- Stakeholder engagement
- Social and business derivatives
- Corporate citizenship behavior

Design-to-value
- Understanding customers
- Perceptual semantics
- Knowledge management
- Personal and Lifetime value
- Customer engagement
- Decision dilemma, loyalty standpoints

Attributes of Design Cube
- Convergence of market-society-values
- Value-based business modelling
- Performance with purpose
- Co-creation and co-evolution
- Customers and stakeholders engagement

Enablers of Design Cube
- Market players
- Key activities
- Motivations
- Organizational design
- Communication

Market

Society

The Design Cube

Value

Figure 1.1 The design cube: Elements and enablers.

Source: Author's analysis.

the attributes of market competition as it increases the market value of corporate cash holdings (Yung and Nguyen 2020). Firms with integrated design-to-market and design-to-society concepts find ways to coevolve with low-cost resources (human capital and technology), train the workers in-house to overcome shortages of skilled employees, and rely on frugal innovations (e.g. Bhattacharya and Michael 2008). These attributes help them scale-up business quickly, avoiding some challenges of rising completion. Firms incubating in the design cube invest in top management talent in order to sustain rapid growth. Marketing by design is an innovation-driven concept that penetrates the target market by developing the competitive differentiation in delivering the products and services. Most profitable strategies focus on differentiation by exploring the latent demand (which explains that customers are unable to find the products they desire) and offer customers strategic values, which competitors are not able to provide. Such business leverage provides the firms near monopolistic situation and ample scope to build customer loyalty. However, most companies concentrate only on the existing demand to market their products and services, and face fragmented market share. Successful companies differentiate their products and services by analyzing the linear elements in the marketing path comprising problems, needs, solutions, perceived values, competitive advantage, and loyalty over time among customers. Such behavioral analysis in the customer-centric firms begin from the moment customers realize they need a product and service but is currently unavailable (MacMillan and McGrath 1997).

The dimensions of social performance of firms suggest that the convergence of market competition and social relationship is discrete. Social performance includes broad business-related public perspectives, such as community welfare, sustainability, human rights, and the social benefits of employees in the firm. Uber practices the design-to-market and design-to society business philosophies by sharing client information and customizing needs on the predetermined technology platform. In this context, the Unilever Sustainable Living Program (USLP) demonstrates a set of bold environmental and social objectives. The USLP has quantified objectives, which are clearly defined, meticulously specified, and independently audited to set design-to-society norms for its brands such as *Lifebuoy*, an antibacterial toilet soap. The USLP has emerged as a social marketing strategy through corporate social responsibility approaches aiming to enhance the brand outreach and gain competitive lead from the challenger brand *Dettol*, manufactured by Reckitt Benckiser India Limited. Both brands are contemplating to grow as social brands by reinforcing design-to-society strategy of marketing. There are some social products like *Jibo Social Robot*, which has prima facie social service attributes and later linked with design-to-market strategies to gain competitive leverage against other absolute commercial brands. The NTT group companies find broad possibilities to bring the social robot to major players in different industries and draw its transition from B2C to corporate environments. The robot has artificial intelligence and expresses a wide range of human-like emotions through sophisticated body movements for communication in a family, social institutions, or in a business organization. It is also used as an educational tool (for guided learning) for children at home and initial school stages. Value co-creation and consumer-brand engagement are integrated brand-building strategies, and they positively influence customers' behavior. The value-based strategies influence building customer satisfaction, consumer-brand relationships, customer retention, brand equity, and competitive advantage. The design-to-value business strategies embed the value-based strategies to gain competitive advantage in the market, converging the design-to-society and design-to-market business philosophies (Pansari and Kumar 2017). Periodical analysis of the following attributes helps firms in understanding behavioral dimensions of customers:

- Perceptions (awareness, self-image congruence, and perceptual semantics)
- Preferences (product attributes, perceived use value, initial knowledge, and motivation)
- Purchase intentions (competitive leverage, price and promotion benefits, buying outlets, and point of sales stimulus), and
- Propensity of buying (volume and frequency of buying).

Analysis of the previous attributes contributes to the firms in developing design-to-value business strategies through enhancement of personal and lifetime values of consumers. Personal values of consumers include anthropomorphism, self-actualization, and self-esteem. The design-to-value strategies of the companies enable them to resolve the dilemma in decision making and loyalty standpoints of the customers. Customer-centric companies develop customer engagement not only to enhance their participation in product development and promotions, but also in evolving the design-to-value strategies in businesses. Design-to-value strategies of the firm enhances the scope of creation and capture of value by engaging customers and stakeholders. Co-creation of products and services provides opportunity to generate value, enhance customer relationships, and cultivate loyalty. Most customer-centric companies tend to create customer value by delivering distinctive values in the niche markets (Yoo and Park 2016). Most companies open up their design-to-value thinking based on experience sharing of customers with products, services, or the consumption chain. It is a co-creation process where customers and firms both uncover opportunities to avail competitive leverage.

The relationship between customers and firms is traditionally managed through a horizontal thrust approach on digital platforms. Social media channels contribute significantly in diffusion of user-generated communication and the corporate point of view on what to sell and how to sell products and services to customers. Such exchange of communications among customers would help firms inculcate customer value and loyalty over time. However, emotional understandings of customers about products and services, and the corporate image influences the customer engagement, buying intentions, and purchasing preferences. Customers are better informed through interactive digital channels where they build high expectations. Nonetheless, the noncongruence between the high expectations and level of satisfaction affect the loyalty of customers (Straker and Wrigley 2016). The key market players including technology providers and supply chain operators are the major enablers of the design cube. These enablers are also engaged in the innovation, value creation, and generating competitive leverage for the firms to gain sustained business growth. The principal motivations that drive firms to strategize and implement the design cube constituents include the growing innovations and technology, market competition, social and personal values, and public policies to some extent. The design cube concept is better evolved in an organization that has employee empowerment and team culture with shared responsibility. In managing the design cube, transparency in communication within and outside the firm affects the value-based relationships among customers, stakeholders, and the firm.

Value System in Society and Market

Market performance of products and services are largely influenced by the social and customer value systems. The value system in the society and market is founded on the philosophy of hierarchy of needs. By analyzing the values associated at various hierarchical levels of human needs, customer-centric firms develop business insights and continue co-creating values with the customers. Such behavior can be described around four types of value systems as discussed next (Almquist et al. 2016):

- Functional value, which generates perceived used value on products and services in the context of utilitarian perspectives
- Emotional values, which are governed by various psychosocial factors including experience sharing, customer interactions, family and societal motivations, quality of life, self-image congruence, and anthropomorphic sensitivity
- Life-changing points in use of products and services like self-actualization and self-esteem (e.g., luxury automobiles, fashion brands, and business class travels), social and economic comparisons, and result-oriented products and services (machines and infrastructure), and
- Social impact on customer psychology and consumption pattern that stimulates emotional and life-changing experiences among customers.

Based on the previous value taxonomy, the use of value-based marketing (VBM) system is growing, and business-to-consumers and business-to-business market segment today typically participate in a diverse value marketing portfolio. Nevertheless, the proportion of total value-centric revenue derived from these segments is usually small as it is an intangible element, which is derived by the cognitive ergonomics (CE) of customers. CE evolves in customers through various touch points including customer personality, self-image congruence, economic stimulants, responsiveness of products and services, and trust in brand and the associated services. Consequently, the management of VBM is a complex phenomenon and has high variability across the geo-demographic and market segments. Design and implementation of VBM system is challenging for most companies despite the potential benefits of VBM strategy. Often, poor communication, transparency, and quality of services affect the value-based formulas and metrics causing inconsistent alignment with customers, market players, and firms. In addition, lack of actionable insights for motivating behavioral changes and suboptimal coordination between various market players, customers, and stakeholders throws challenges to the firms. The successful experiences of the customer-centric and industrial marketing companies indicate that bringing the social values within the proximity of markets provides enhanced scope to implement VBM strategies and inculcate systems thinking in value management process. Therefore, multinational customer-centric companies build shared values in the market to benefit customers by serving both the social and personal values of customers.

Most customer-centric (Nestlé, Unilever, IKEA, SC Johnson, etc.) and industrial marketing companies (General Electric, Cisco, General Motors, and the like) are able to bring business and society together through stakeholder engagement, corporate social responsibility, and public–private partnerships. These firms have redefined their social business purpose as creating shared value to not only generate economic value but also co-create the need-based solutions in the society addressing its challenges. In order to develop corporate social values, firms tend to categorically revive products and markets to fit to the social needs; reconstruct manufacturing, marketing, and services value chains; and build servitization clusters at various social and commercial destinations. Most large firms have set up such initiatives. Nestlé, for example, redesigned its coffee procurement process by providing on-farm consultations to farmers on agricultural practices, helping them in plant protection measures and application of fertilizers and pesticides, and giving them a competitive price for the coffee beans. Consequently, farmers have experienced higher yields and income from the coffee plantation. Nestlé has implemented such program in Columbia and Brazil as corporate social responsibility program. The social impact of intervention of Nestlé in agribusiness has improved the ecological conservation in coffee farming and augmented the supply of good coffee beans in the region. The efforts of Nestlé through corporate social responsibility program has not only created the shared value but also triggered market capitalism (Porter and Kramer 2011). The ecosystems of the shared values, which converge the social and business goals to improve performance of products and services of a firm in the competitive marketplace, are detailed as follows (e.g. Kramer and Pfitzer 2016):

- Commonality in corporate and social goals, which helps in aligning the stakeholders and defines their commitment (Jonnalagedda and Saranga 2017)
- Developing a measurement system for shared accountability and values that contributes to the implementation of corporate social responsibility programs
- Public–private initiatives to mutually implement social business development programs and reinforce human values alongside of business goals
- Ensuring consistency and transparency in communication to build trust in business activities, and
- Developing social support for business to deliver social products and services and mobilizes resources toward public–private partnership projects and programs.

The shared values help firms restructure their organizational capabilities to create trust among the stakeholders, customers, and market players. Trust reinforces knowledge (awareness) and wisdom (rationality) in planning and implementation of business strategies. The level of confidence among the employees of the firm and the market players including investors, supply chain partners, technology providers, marketers, and customers help firms in streamlining the coordinating mechanisms to the business scalable. The shared values guide managers at different levels in the organization on developing shared business strategies aiming to achieve business goals together with the society and market. Cohesive customer values cultivate a code of contribution to delineate the common purpose of society–business collaborations. Customer-centric companies

develop scalable business by coordinating people's efforts and coopetition (cooperative competition), which prompts the firms to enhance performance in the marketplace (Adler et al. 2011). Walmart, the largest
retailer in North America, has strengthened its competitive advantage by
creating shared value among customers in an attempt to lead against the
brick-and-mortar and virtual retailers and keep customers satisfied with
growing demands. The shared value in Walmart is all about customer
supremacy and trust on the services rendered by the firms. Such value
measure has enhanced the scope of the firms to develop customer-centric
strategy in fending off competition, easing the navigation a challenging in
retail landscape, and positioning Walmart as a leading retailer.

Similarly, Nestlé is also engaged in creating shared value as principal
business strategy by focusing on educating customers and serving to the
community goals on the nutrition, water, and rural development sectors.
In the packaged food and beverage industry, social pressure has been
increasing toward restructuring sustainability in the supply chain value
management and serve the social health goals set under public policies
in various countries. Putting the society first in business planning, Nestlé
has transformed in the product manufacturing, marketing, and services
objectives to provide a healthy basket of foods. The shared values have
transformed the product portfolios of the company to cater to the social
well-being goals at the forefront. Over time, the company could successfully embed the shared-values strategy as the corporate policy integrated
with the social value and communicated to its stakeholders (e.g. Porter
et al. 2015). Such strategy of Nestlé has satisfactorily converged the triadic
facets of its business model with design-to-market, design-to-society, and
design-to-value perspectives. The attributes of value system in society and
market are illustrated in Figure 1.2.

The customers' and stakeholders' values are embedded in the social
ecosystem, which is founded on the culture, ethnicity, and collective intelligence within and outside the community. The applied social thinking,
which stimulates social values, is based on the linear process of recognizing problems, needs, and solutions by corporate firms. Consequently, the
value system emerges out of the social and economic indicators, which
affects businesses and their *performance with purpose*. The taxonomy of
value system includes the attributes of learned value, acquired value, and
interrelated value as illustrated in Figure 1.2. Learned values are grown

• Social Institutions
• Corporate Social Responsibility
• PubliePrivate Partnership
• Sustainability Goals
• Social Innovations

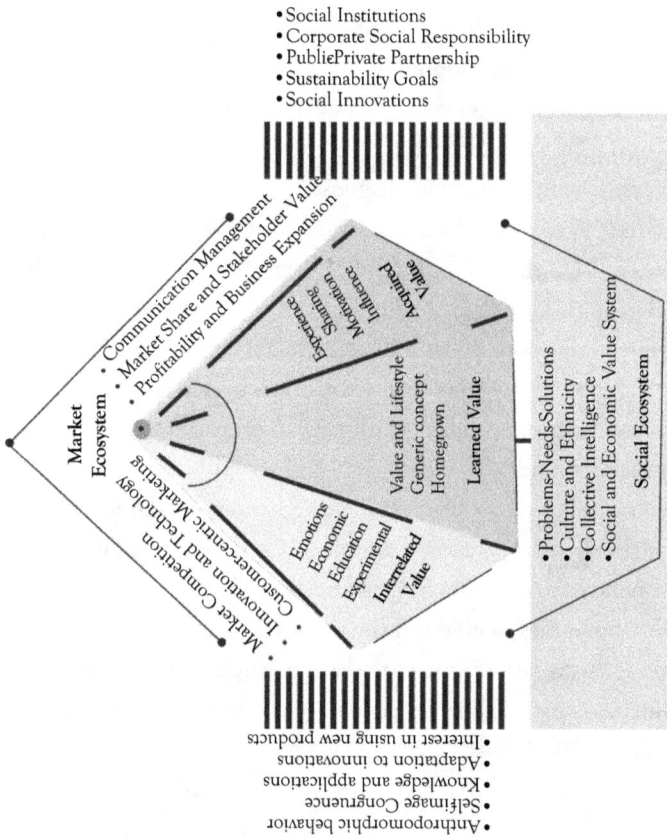

Figure 1.2 The value ecosystems in society and market scenarios

Source: Author

in the society or within the family, and customers are adapted to such values which are hard to alter. Such values are generic in nature and vary by society, community, or clans to which customers belong. The learned values also determine the lifestyle of customers. Companies focusing on marketing of social or learned values-based products and services need to understand the social culture, ethnicity, and consumption pattern before getting started with the customer-centric business. Boehringer Ingelheim (BI), a German-based multinational pharmaceutical company in Mexico, has been engaged in developing its business in convergence with the increasing social consciousness on services-driven product marketing. BI is discretely operating the patients service centers (in Spanish *Centro Atencion de Pacientes*), which offer free diagnostic services (only for referred patients) leading to support clinical diagnosis of the patients. The diagnostic services of BI at the aforementioned centers include the data analysis of arterial pressure ambulatory monitors, cardiovascular monitors, and respirators. Such services of BI are indirectly linked with the marketing of pharmaceutical products of the company through prescriptions. Linking of social services with the product marketing thus creates social value of BI pharmaceutical brands.

Customers acquire values from strong external market influences and experience sharing among fellow customers. Commonly acquired values play temporary stimulus among customers toward buying. It takes a long time for companies to establish the acquired values as the drivers of decision among customers. Experience sharing, internal motivation, and external influence constitute the key elements in forming the acquired values among customers. The 4Es comprising emotions, economic complementarity, education and undated knowledge, and experimental behavior inculcate interrelated values among consumers toward their association with relevant products and services (Awate et al. 2015). Exploring interrelated values helps firms analyze the suitability of launching new products and brand extensions in the new or existing consumer segments. The value incentives encourage social value-led firms to develop syncretic stewardship, which drives firms on socialization of business through corporate social responsibility programs.

The growing market competition across geo-demographic segments due to increasing effects of innovation and technology has systematically affected the market share and stakeholder values of customer-centric firms. Growth in frugal innovations, increasing concerns of consumers on utilitarian use value, and adaptability to innovation and technology have significantly contributed to the market ecosystem. The extensive adaptation to technology and digital media has set the new consumption pattern of consumer products and services. Online platforms have succeeded at drawing attention of customers toward innovative products by highlighting the peer evaluations, preferences, and purchase intentions. However, there is a dynamic shift strategic moves of the firms in the recent year (year 2001 and ahead) toward new market ecosystems built on digital marketing, competitive dynamics, market research, brand footprint analysis, process and product innovations, customer value system, and market segmentation. The social institutions nurture social innovations though public–private partnership and participating corporate social responsibility programs (Dass and Kumar 2014). Such social engagement of customers and stakeholders enable the social value system to grow along side of market ecosystem. In addition, consumer behavior (anthropomorphic and self-image congruence) stimulates the interest new products, ease-of-use perception, and adaptation of emerging innovations. Consequently, social ecosystem and market systems contribute significantly in business modeling for customer-centric companies (Cajaiba-Santana 2014).

Systems Thinking in Business

Systems consist of people, structures, technologies, and processes that work together to make organizations viable. Systems thinking, a part of operations and management research, essentially looks at the whole as a basis for understanding, designing, and managing its components. Systems thinking is applied in organizational management for decades in the field of operations, but it has also been conceptualized in the functional areas of marketing. Systems thinking offers a powerful new perspective, a synchronized flow of thoughts, and a set of tools that can be used to address the most complex problems in everyday business operations. Systems thinking may be considered as a way of understanding reality that emphasizes the relationships among various components in a process, rather than the independent constituents of the process. Based on a field of study known as system dynamics, systems thinking have a practical value that rests on a solid theoretical foundation. In marketing operations, systems thinking can be described as a tool in tracing and linking various activities in a particular function. To be competitive, companies must develop innovative new businesses on competitive market platforms. Firms may face several operational barriers and seldom mesh smoothly with well-established systems, processes, and cultures. Nonetheless, success requires a balance of conventional and new marketing strategies to keep the competitive forces in equilibrium (Garvin and Levesque 2006). Emerging companies face various challenges when they pursue new businesses and the usual problematic responses to those challenges. The systems thinking is usually driven by many small systems or subsystems. For example, an organization is made up of many administrative and management functions, products, services, groups, and individuals. If one part of the system is changed, the nature of the overall system is often changed as well by definition. Systems theory has brought a new perspective for managers to interpret the patterns and events in their organizations.

Interactivity of customers, stakeholders, and other market players within the backward and forward operations has been actively encouraged by the companies through social media and corporate channels. Various interactive digital platforms today have created close proximity among these players and enabled them to collaborate in decision-making process by sharing designs, experiences, and emotions. Interactive design is both the art of finding differences among things that seem similar and the science of finding similarities among things that seem different. The distinct outputs of interactive design may lead to defining problems, identifying the leverage point and designing solutions-ideation process. Interactive design is a part of critical thinking that is determined by defining a problem, gathering of information for problem solution, formulation of hypotheses, checking presumptions, and correctness of findings, making a solution. Interactive design offers a constant critical assessment, and continuous learning and understanding of mental models. This dimension of systems thinking is based on intuitive thinking that stimulates creativity and provides an organization with a conceptual foundation to create a unique competitive advantage. The elements of systems thinking as drivers of in decision making in business are exhibited in Figure 1.3.

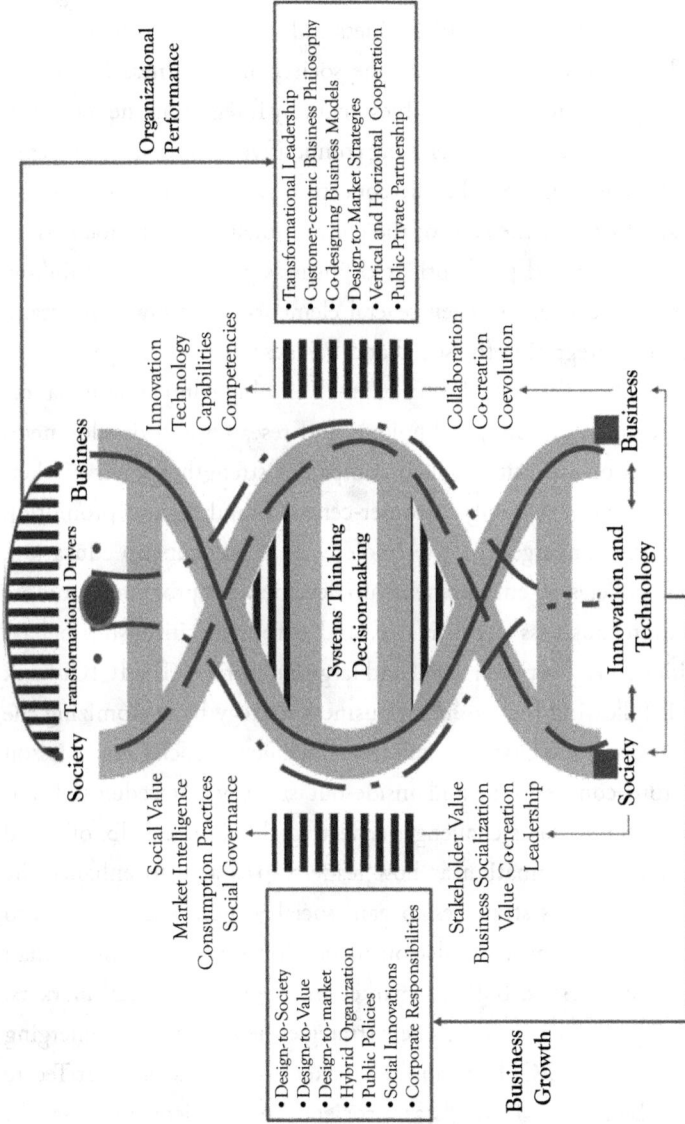

Figure 1.3 Systems thinking in business and societal strategies

Source: Author.

Figure 1.3 illustrates that the success of systems thinking approach needs a transformational leadership at both business organizations to help in redesigning organization, creating value chain, developing global standards, investing in business process improvement, and strengthening the backward and forward business linkages. The business growth exhibits building synergy between the society and business firms. The concept of synergy refers to the achievement by integrating the social values with business goals for developing competitiveness, trust among consumers, and ensuring growth. The concept drives the firms to make an additional effort over the sum of the conventional decisions focused on market leadership and profit-oriented business goals. Systems thinking stimulates cooperation between several elements and allows for greater overall effects integrating the social and business values (Carayannis and Campbell 2009). The coevolution of small and big companies enhances investment on innovation, technology, and research and development. Such mergers or acquisitions help companies strengthen their marketing strategies by developing customer-centric branding and promotion strategies. The convergence of technology, entrepreneurship education, and public policies on entrepreneurship development programs promote hybridization, business performance, and corporate citizenship behavior ambidextrously between small and large enterprises. The ICICI bank of India is following the *outside-in* business strategy by customizing the products and services based on collective intelligence, social needs, lesson learned from competition, and inside-out strategy antecedents. Leadership in business poses challenges reflecting the double helix of social and business transformation as how leadership is able to enhance the effectiveness business strategies to gain social values. The bank is also intending to evolve as a social icon to develop a wider portfolio than the existing business-to-business market and lead the financial markets. By managing the social and business strategies helix effect, the emerging giants such as the ICICI bank and the maker of the Mexican beer Tecate are able to build global brands as a societal business icon (Kumar and Steenkamp 2013).

The 5-T determinants lay the groundwork for success inside the new organization. The typical work culture of 5-T power grid may be described as synergy of task (commitment), thrust (driving force), time (punctuality), target (customers by segments), and trust (value perceptions). These attributes of the Japanese distinguish them from most of the existing work cultures across the countries in the world. This has reflected into the material culture (technology and economy) of Japan toward continues improvement (Kaizen). In fact, Kaizen is a social culture, which has been later adopted by the Japanese organizations. These indicators serve as drivers of systems thinking in business. An appropriate convergence of these factors has made the business firms stronger and sustainable during the economic recessions. It is observed that knowledge management fully mediates the impact of organizational culture on organizational effectiveness, and partially mediates the impact of organizational structure and strategy on organizational effectiveness. There is a possible mediating role of knowledge management in managing relationship between the systems thinking attributes comprising organizational goals, employee engagement, stakeholder values, work culture, decision-making process, and organizational effectiveness (Zheng et al. 2010).

Business Transformation

Transition, transformation, and transactions in business modeling are interrelated and constitute a linear path to the business performance of firms in the competitive marketplace. Shifting from conventional wisdom to contemporary business philosophies is a clear transition for many companies in both business-to-consumers and business-to-business segments. However, transiting from one business culture (leader oriented) to another (stakeholder focused) is a major challenge for companies. In the transition process, firms need to integrate employees, stakeholders, business processes, operative platforms, and change management in the context of mergers and acquisitions; and restore the internal organizational values. The transformation from the conventional business to the digital interface began by the end of the 20 century in the Thomson Corporation. With the advancement of digital business in the newspaper market segment, the company realized that it needed to bridge the critical business gap and began the transition process. The company began systematically scrutinizing its end users and as part of a new front-end customer strategy; the change would become the cornerstone of the firm's transformation. In the first round of transition, the company adopted a user-centric approach initially in the Thomson Financial division and later moved the change management throughout the organization. Redefining the market of the company, which was mapped not by type of purchaser but by end-user segments, provided a clear view of the division's real, addressable market and of corresponding opportunities. After understanding the user preferences, Thomson Corporation has charted their entire workflow and identified the needed values that could be added to the transiting business process. Later, through cluster and conjoint analysis, the company determined how product preferences varied among the users. The company has changed radically over time (Harrignton and Tjan 2008).

The transformation of business model is a holistic process from amending the corporate philosophy to manufacturing and marketing process of the product and services. Transformation process includes employee engagement, decision making, internal and external relationships, backward and forward linkages and, and optimizing the resources management. Transformation of a business model can be linked to a new technology with focus on an emerging market. It needs to transform the consumption behavior and the current industry approach of marketing the products and services to realize a holistic view of transformation of business in an industry. Apple revolutionized the market for audio devices by integrating iPod with iTunes. But most attempts to introduce a new model often failed to fully transform the market. The transformation of business model based on the following strategies lead to a near success:

- Customization of products and services (Dell computers in the initial business model adapted to the customization of products to gain customer value and lead the market nonconventionally)
- Closed-loop marketing process (connecting customers, suppliers, value added resellers, original equipment manufacturers, and service providers)
- Asset sharing among collaborators (to encourage co-creation and enhanced creativity)

- Consumption-based pricing (utilitarian pricing model to provide "value for money" sensitivity among customers)
- A collaborative ecosystem (to grow as an agile, shared value, and socially adaptive organization).

The prior strategies may strengthen the transformation move of the companies that are thinking about changing their business model or entering an industry with a new model in the competitive marketplace (Kavadias et al. 2016). The transformation of traditional firms is slow as they change the process step-by-step instead of attempting a radical move. The emerging firms tend to exploit their greater resources and knowledge and explore a variety of ideas in a sequential process. Firms tend to transform the business processes by developing digital technology, co-creating value-based products and services, analyzing collective intelligence, building shared values, and minimizing organizational risks in change management (Un and Rodríguez 2018).

Best Buy, an American departmental store, has transformed its organizational culture and marketing strategies for striking back at Amazon. Best Buy renovated its business processes that enabled the firm to minimize costs and introduce competitive prices, and develop its stores into as an e-commerce hub to entertain online orders and store pickups. The company also reoriented its employees on customer-relation approaches, and fixed accountability in the frontline employees to strengthen the customer values for both online and instore transactions (McGrath and McManus 2020). Similarly, Office Depot, an American office stationary and equipment supplier, has planned transformation of their business by comprehensively understanding customer preferences and values. The company has developed a rebranding campaign focusing on consumer awareness about the current office supply trends and their needs. Office Depot scheduled a series of training programs for its employees toward acquiring new customers and retaining those existing in both business-to-consumers and business-to-business market segments. The company also restructured integration of supply chain, systems integration, and the existing brick-and-mortar stores to overcome competitive supply threats from local office stationary suppliers. The periodical customer information from mystery shoppers (covert employees of the company, who pretend as customers, to learn the feelings of the customers and also get information from competing channels in disguise) helped the company analyze customer service score. The company learned about the significance of customer observation on various instore factors, such as cleanliness of floors and bathrooms, which were underplayed by the company. In the business transformation process, Office Depot had developed plans of employee empowerment to create internal values and are incentivized in catering to the customer services in generating right value perspectives (Peters 2011).

The information technology and the popularity of social media have empowered companies in collecting and analyzing data on the key indicators of consumer behavior to map their problems, needs, preferences, and consumption practices. Nonetheless, most market-oriented firms need to shift their focus from driving transactional business models to value-based business models to gain competitive leverage and maximize customer lifetime value. In the value-based business model, products and brands must be made subservient to customer relationships transforming the marketing by nurturing customers rather than thrusting products, adopting new performance metrics, and bringing market players under a single customer-centric marketing umbrella. The corporate transformation can be better managed by understanding about personal resilience on change management strategy of the company, the contribution of innovation and technology in marketing new products, and reorienting customer interest in adapting to the new portfolios of products and services (Rust et al. 2010). Managing change in organizations needs a critical balance between the new strategies, emotions of customers, and market response to the transformation.

Transforming markets for adapting to product and services innovations is a big challenge for most companies engaged in doing business in consumer products. Innovative products need to be transformed to the perceived suitability of consumers for optimal use by way of total customization. Most innovative products have the limitation for 360° transformation due to the standardized functionality and built-in structural restrictions. Driving change in the demand and consumer behavior has traditionally influenced the top-down initiatives such as corporate endorsements toward manufacturing design, quality, and technology. For example, light emitting diode (LED) screens and lighting devices have transformed the consumer behavior and market demand to get more value at less price. Companies can develop strategies of innovation launch and transformation to stimulate consumer preferences. To work with such strategies, companies need to consider the following attributes (Rajagopal 2020b):

- Co-create community orientation in business
- Engage in the business process exploring innovative products and services to gain competitive benefits and value for money
- Plan for strategic transformation through understanding customer needs, values, and market response
- Involve in expansion of the existing channel network to market solution-led innovative products
- Encourage direct marketing practices to create customer value
- Plan for transfer of knowledge, technology, and innovation values among customers and market players by creating constructive learning platforms
- Nurture communication grapevine through the digital networks and customer communities on the contributions of innovations and competitive advantages
- Disseminate awareness on innovations as solutions to the social and customer problems to the deliver social value
- Leverage social, economic, market-based, and customers' evidence on transformed strategies and transacted products and services
- Build immunity to innovations in the market against disruptions and misevaluations that could build low trust and commitment among the consumers and market players.

Companies should ensure that throughout the previous steps, they must adopt a facilitator's role without overpowering the consumers or raising conflicts with the competitors. Such corporate attitude may cause damage to the brand image of the company. The customer-centric innovation transformation methodology can help in solving even the most extreme dilemmas on innovation acceptability in the market and its socialization for sustained growth (Pascale and Sternin 2005). Transformational business models have become the essential success parameters of any business. Vertical and horizontal integrations are imperative to the success of a corporation, resulting in the models that provide tremendous business opportunities. These approaches also bring great execution challenges.

Summary

Strategic thinking helps new entrants adjust their ecosystem with the factors that influence one another in a cycle that stimulates the management of the design cube comprising design-to-market, design-to-society, and design-to-value. The business ecosystem is fundamentally based on these triadic design pillars. Continuous learning and exploring ways to catch-up with industry changes drive firms to stay agile with the dynamic business ecosystems. Industrial marketing firms have moved today from relationship management goals to ecosystem orchestration process. The business ecosystems help firms in text mining and analyzing collective intelligence. The emphasis on co-creation of innovation gradually generates technological breakthroughs. Such shift in the business philosophy has encouraged the role of collective intelligence in building customer-centric strategies and co-creating customer-centric innovations to develop standalone posture in the competitive marketplace. The technological adaptation in businesses broadly supports the design-cube perspectives in the context of design-to-market, design-to-society, and design-to-value strategies. Business models are built around triadic constituents including market (competition), society (social needs, responsibility, and sustainability), and values (customers and stakeholders). These elements are integrated to explain the design cube through design-to-market, design-to-society, and design-to-value perspectives in contemporary business modeling process.

The shared values help firms restructure their organizational capabilities to create trust among the stakeholders, customers, and market players. The systems thinking fits aptly to the design cube concept of business modeling by converging design-to-market, design-to-society, and design-to-value perspectives. Shifting from conventional wisdom to contemporary business philosophies is a clear transition for many companies in both business-to-consumers and business-to-business segments. In the transition process, firms need to integrate employees, stakeholders, business processes, operative platforms, change management in the context of mergers and acquisitions, and restore the internal organizational values.

References

Adler, P., C. Heckscher, and L. Prusak. 2011. "Building a Collaborative Enterprise." *Harvard Business Review* 89, nos. 7–8, pp. 94–101.

Almquist, E., J. Senior, and N. Bloch. 2016. "The Elements of Value." *Harvard Business Review* 94, no. 9, pp. 47–53.

Awate, S., M.M. Larsen, and R. Mudambi. 2015. "Accessing vs Sourcing Knowledge: A Comparative Study of R&D Internationalization between Emerging and Advanced Economy Firms." *Journal of International Business Studies* 46, no. 1, pp. 63–86.

Bhattacharya, A.K., and D.C. Michael. 2008. "How Local Companies Keep Multinationals at Bay." *Harvard Business Review* 86, no. 3, pp. 84–95.

Birkinshaw, J. 2019. "Ecosystem Businesses Are Changing the Rules of Strategy." *Harvard Business Review Digital Article.*

Cajaiba-Santana, G. 2014. "Social Innovation: Moving the Field Forward. A Conceptual Framework." *Technology Forecasting and Social Change* 82, no. 1, pp. 42–51.

Carayannis, E.G., and M. Zedtwitz. 2005. "Architecting GloCal (Global–Local), Real-Virtual Incubator Networks (G-RVINs) as Catalysts and Accelerators of Entrepreneurship in Transitioning and Developing Economies: Lessons Learned and Best Practices from Current Development and Business Incubation Practices." *Technovation* 25, no. 2, pp. 95–110.

Carayannis, E.G., and D.F. Campbell. 2009. "Mode 3′ and 'Quadruple Helix': Toward a 21st Century Fractal Innovation Ecosystem." *International Journal of Technology and Management* 46, no. 3–4, pp. 201–234.

Dass, M., and S. Kumar. 2014. "Bringing Product and Consumer Ecosystems to the Strategic Forefront." *Business Horizons* 57, no. 2, pp. 225–234.

Elia, G., A. Margherita, and G. Passiante. 2020. "Digital Entrepreneurship Ecosystem: How Digital Technologies and Collective Intelligence Are Reshaping the Entrepreneurial Process." *Technological Forecasting and Social Change* 150. https://doi.org/10.1016/j.techfore.2019.119791

Esch, P., D. Arli, M.H. Gheshlaghi, V. Andonopoulos, T. Heidt, and G. Northey. 2019. "Anthropomorphism and Augmented Reality in the Retail Environment." *Journal of Retailing and Consumer Services* 49, no. 1, pp. 35–42.

Garvin, D.A., and L.C. Levesque. 2006. "Meeting Challenges of the Corporate Entrepreneurship." *Harvard Business Review* 84, no. 10, pp. 102–110.

Giones, F., and A. Brem. 2017. "Digital Technology Entrepreneurship: A Definition and Research Agenda." *Technology and Innovation Management Review* 7, no. 5, pp. 44–51.

Guimaraes, P.P., and P. Chandon. 2004. *Unilever in Brazil 1997–2007: Marketing Strategies for Low-Income Consumers*. Boston: Harvard Business School Publication.

Harrignton, R.J., and A.K. Tjan. 2008. "Transforming Strategy One Customer at a Time." *Harvard Business Review* 86, no. 3, pp. 62–72.

Jacobides, M.G. 2019. "In the Ecosystem Economy, What's Your Strategy?" *Harvard Business Review Digital Article*.

Jonnalagedda, S., and H. Saranga. 2017. "Commonality Decisions When Designing for Multiple Markets." *European Journal of Operational Research* 258, no. 3, pp. 902–911.

Kanter, R.M. 2012. "Enriching the Ecosystem." *Harvard Business Review* 90, no. 3, pp. 140–147.

Kavadias, S., K. Ladas, and C.H. Loch. 2016. "The Transformative Business Model." *Harvard Business Review* 94, no. 10, pp. 91–98.

Kramer, M.R., and M. Pfitzer. 2016. "The Ecosystem of Shared Value." *Harvard Business Review* 94, no. 10, pp. 80–89.

Kuester, S., E. Konya-Baumbach, and M.C. Schuhmacher. 2018. "Get the Show on the Road: Go-to-Market Strategies for e-Innovations of Start-Ups." *Journal of Business Research* 83, no. 1, pp. 65–81.

Kumar, N., and J.E.M. Steenkamp. 2013. "Diaspora Marketing." *Harvard Business Review* 91, no. 10, pp. 127–131.

Leung, C.H., and W.T. Yan-Chan. 2020. "Retail Chatbots: The Challenges and Opportunities of Conversational Commerce." *Journal of Digital & Social Media Marketing* 8, no. 1, pp. 68–84.

Liao, Z., and X. Shi. 2009. "Consumer Perceptions of Internet-Based e-Retailing: An Empirical Research in Hong Kong." *Journal of Services Marketing* 23, no. 1, pp. 24–30.

MacMillan, I.C., and R.G. McGrath. 1997. "Discovering New Points of Differentiation." *Harvard Business Review* 75, no. 4, pp. 133–142.

McGrath, R., and R. McManus. 2020. "Discovery-Driven Digital Transformation." *Harvard Business Review Digital Article*. Boston: Harvard Business School Publishing.

Miotti, L., and F. Sachwald. 2003. "Cooperative R&D: Why and with Whom? An Integrated Framework of Analysis." *Research Policy* 32, no. 6, pp. 1481–1499.

Ortiz-Villajos, J.M., and S. Sotoca. 2018. "Innovation and Business Survival: A Long-Term Approach." *Research Policy* 47, no. 8, pp. 1418–1436.

Palepu, K.G., and T. Bijlani. 2012. *Bharti Airtel in Africa*. Boston: Harvard Business School Press.

Pansari, A., and V. Kumar. 2017. "Customer Engagement: The Construct, Antecedents, and Consequences." *Journal of Academy of Marketing Science* 45, no. 3, pp. 294–311.

Parente, R.C., J.M.G. Geleilate, and K. Rong. 2018. "The Sharing Economy Globalization Phenomenon: A Research Agenda." *Journal of International Management* 24, no. 1, pp. 52–64.

Pascale, R.T., and J. Sternin. 2005. "Your Company's Secret Change Agents." *Harvard Business Review* 83, no. 5, pp. 72–81.

Peters, K. 2011. "Office Depot's President on How 'Mystery Shopping' Helped Spark a Turnaround." *Harvard Business Review* 89, no. 11, pp. 47–50.

Porter, M.E., and M.R. Kramer. 2011. "Creating Shared Value." *Harvard Business Review* 89, nos. 1–2, pp. 62–77.

Porter, M.E., M.R. Kramer, K. Herman, and S. McAra. 2015. *Nestle's Creating Shared Value Strategy*. Boston: Harvard Business School Publication.

Quelch, J.A., and E.J. Hoff. 1986. "Customizing Global Marketing." *Harvard Business Review* 64, no. 3, pp. 59–68.

Rajagopal. 2019. "Convergence of Local Enterprises with Large Corporations: Bridging Industry 4.0 Functions on Broader Business Canvas." In *Innovation, Technology, and Market Ecosystem: Managing Industrial Growth in Emerging Markets*, eds. Rajagopal and R. Behl. New York, NY: Palgrave Macmillan.

Rajagopal, and R. Behl. 2020a. *Entrepreneurship and Regional Development: Analyzing Growth Models in Emerging Markets*. New York: Palgrave Macmillan.

Rajagopal. 2020b. *Market Entropy: How to Manage Chaos and Uncertainty for Improving Organizational Performance*. New York: Business Expert Press.

Reeves, M., K. Haanaes, and J. Sinha. 2015. "Navigating the Dozens of Different Strategy Options." *Harvard Business Review* 93, no. 6, pp. 1–17.

Rust, R.T., C. Moorman, and G. Bhalla. 2010. "Rethinking Marketing." *Harvard Business Review* 88, no. 1, pp. 94–101.

Straker, K., and C. Wrigley. 2016. "Designing an Emotional Strategy: Strengthening Digital Channel Engagements." *Business Horizons* 59, no. 3, pp. 339–346.

Un, C.A., and A. Rodríguez. 2018. "Local and Global Knowledge Complementarity: R&D Collaborations and Innovation of Foreign and Domestic Firms." *Journal of International Management* 24, no. 2, pp. 137–152.

Williamson, P., and A. De Meyer. 2019. "How to Monetize a Business Ecosystem." *Harvard Business Review Digital Article*. Boston: Harvard Business School Press.

Yoo, J., and M. Park. 2016. "The Effects of E-Mass Customization on Consumer Perceived Value, Satisfaction, and Loyalty toward Luxury Brands." *Journal of Business Research* 69, no. 12, pp. 5775–5784.

Yung, K., and T. Nguyen. 2020. "Managerial Ability, Product Market Competition, and Firm Behavior." *International Review of Economics and Finance* 70, no. 1, pp. 102–116.

Zahra, S.A., and S. Nambisan. 2012. "Entrepreneurship and Strategic Thinking in Business Ecosystems." *Business Horizons* 55, no. 3, pp. 219–229.

Zellweger, T.M., J.J. Chrisman, J.H. Chua, and L.P. Steier. 2019. "Social Structures, Social Relationships, and Family Firms." *Entrepreneurship Theory and Practice* 43, no. 2, pp. 207–223.

Zheng, W., B. Yang, and G.N. McLean. 2010. "Linking Organizational Culture, Structure, Strategy, and Organizational Effectiveness: Mediating Role of Knowledge Management." *Journal of Business Research* 63, no. 7, pp. 763–771.

CHAPTER 2

Design-to-Market

Overview

This chapter discusses design-to-market strategy and explains the attributes and ecosystem of marketing and design-thinking process needed to gain competitive leverage and enhance business performance. The hybrid marketing mix comprises innovation and technology, and various contemporary management perspectives to optimize the effects of strategy design in marketing. The design-to-market perspectives have been discussed in the context of developing a strategy map with the elements of marketing mix. In continuation to the discussion on design-to-market concepts, the chapter discusses the convergence of consumer behavior and design strategy by illustrating the strategy wheel phenomenon with a gyroscope metaphor. In addition, the discussion on co-creation and collective intelligence, new product development, and stage gate process adds value in understanding the design-to-market concepts holistically.

Market competition is a dynamic process stimulated by continuous growth in innovation and technology. The changing market competition affects the consumption pattern and behavior of various segments of customers. Consequently, market trends and consumer behavior are continuously changing, and social media is playing a critical role in determining marketing decisions. However, when uncertainty caused by entropy dominates, understanding market volatility is vital. Volatility of customer markets can have significant negative effects on risk-averse market share, profitability, and brand equity of companies. However, volatility is one of the most important concepts in competitive growth theory. The central argument to this theory is that the companies operating in a competitive business environment consider customer preferences, innovation, technology, and growth-related investments. Emerging markets are facing value-based competition as the value-for-money customer segment is expanding latitudinally. The niche players and global retailers are gaining leverage by making flexible business models within economic and political volatility. The agile business models are able to generate shared value among market players, which has become a key indicator of organizational capability. However, local competitors gain greater advantage in leading the market against the national and global companies as these firms serve customers within close proximity and understand the four Ps, the attributes of customers comprising preferences, perceptions, purchase intentions, and psychodynamics (peer interactions, social media communications, and collective intelligence), which affect the buying behavior in general. Local firms avoid mainstream market competition and grow in the niche market because of following reasons (e.g., Bhattacharya and Michael 2008):

- Local firms customize products and services contextual to local needs.
- The customization to local needs restricts firms from scaling of their business.
- Business modeling of niche-based firms is short-term oriented.
- Firms face resource limitations in achieving market competitiveness.
- Most operational problems with local firms are market-specific obstacles.
- Competing firms reorient their businesses on latest technologies to enhance organizational capabilities and competence.
- The human capital in local firms are trained in-house to meet the needs of skilled employees at low cost.
- Local firms are supported by the public policies and social values.
- Patronage from the government and social institutions helps local firms scale-up their business before facing the challenges of market competition.
- Local firms invest in transformational leadership to sustain rapid growth in competitive marketplace.

Market competition is driven by the continuous innovation and technology, which affect the consumption behavior significantly.

Most firms build their competitiveness by positioning frugal innovation products with low-cost and high-value strategy. The success of frugal innovation products often attracts large companies, which have capabilities to co-create and coevolve frugal and niche-based innovations for upscaling and commercialization. Looking beyond innovation and technology, shifts from the single-retailer model to a multiretailer model has boosted market competition, which has affected market stability. Multiplicity of marketing functions like manufacturing and distribution has significantly contributed to chaos in the market. Congestion of firms in competitive marketplace can be visualized in the mobile phone industry of China, which focuses *one supplier and one bounded-retailer* rationale. Consequently, most manufacturers follow a similar marketing and distribution pattern as the single-retailer model is extended to a multiretailer approach, which has augmented the market competition manifold (Rajagopal 2020).

Design-to-Market Strategy

Customer-centric companies tend to use value-based strategic tools and processes, which are co-created in collaboration with customers, stakeholders, and key business partners. The value-based strategies help firms measure the magnitude of business within the geo-demographic segment and the marketplace (premium, mass, niche, or bottom-of-the pyramid) to revise and reinforce the marketing strategies. Firms build organizational structures to proactively lead customers considering the rationale of their buying decision to purchase and beyond. Accordingly, companies engineer *design-to-market* strategies by mapping behavioral journeys of customers to gain competitive advantage for their products and services against other players. Building successful design-to-market strategies requires the following capabilities of the customer-centric business firms:

- Managing smooth transition of the organizational philosophy of the firm from *marketing-to-customers* to *marketing-with-customers* considering them as business associates
- Building need-based and solution-led product portfolios in the marketplace to generate customer value

- Adapting to a comprehensive marketing mix to develop appropriate strategies than narrowing down the key strategy indicators
- Creating a customized experience by overriding the dissatisfaction of customers on total or near-total standardization of products and services
- Synchronization of contextual interactions with customers and key business partners (suppliers, advertisers, promotors, and service providers)
- Analyzing customers' feedback and learning to manager future strategies systematically
- Mapping sequential steps to develop differentiation among the products and services in the marketplace
- Mapping customer journey to understand the linear and critical paths to their buying decision making, and
- Fostering customer loyalty by creating lifetime value.

Successful companies have a precise organizational structure, with an accountable manager and a strategist to map customer journey and earmark prominent touchpoints to consider while building a competitive marketing strategy. This practice helps firms in developing design-to-market strategy and planning for desired business performance in the competitive marketplace (Eldelman and Singer 2015). The ecosystem of the *design-to-market* strategy and discussed the core and peripheral determinants is exhibited in Figure 2.1.

Design-to-market has emerged as a contemporary business philosophy and stimulated firms to develop strategies compatible to the target market. The underlying principle of design-to-market philosophy is to co-create products and services and develop communications through user-generated content to deliver value to the target customers and generate incremental profit. The hexagonal model of design-to-market philosophy illustrates the six core strategy areas comprising decision making, organizational control, functional factors, market attributes and competition, social interface of business, and co-creation as exhibited in Figure 2.1. These areas are dynamic and firms use transformational approaches to optimize their effects

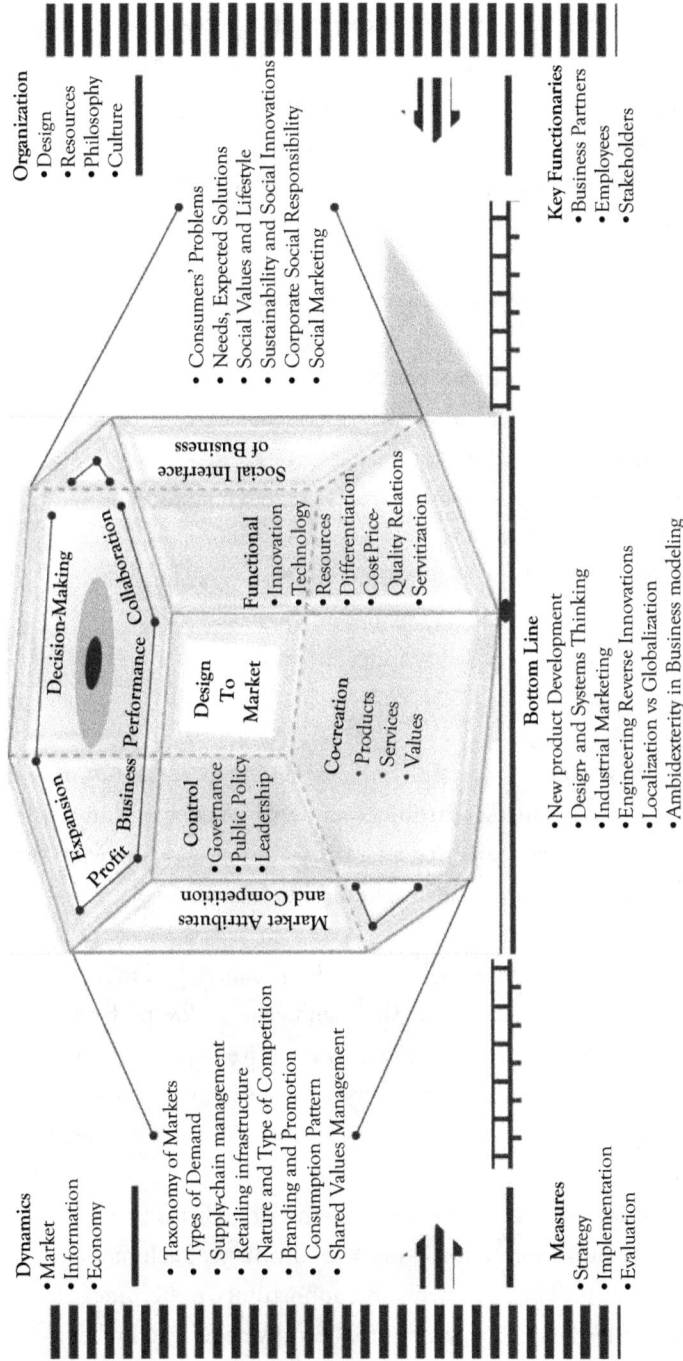

Organization
- Design
- Resources
- Philosophy
- Culture

Key Functionaries
- Business Partners
- Employees
- Stakeholders

- Consumers' Problems
- Needs, Expected Solutions
- Social Values and Lifestyle
- Sustainability and Social Innovations
- Corporate Social Responsibility
- Social Marketing

Social Interface of Business

Functional
- Innovation
- Technology
- Resources
- Differentiation
- Cost Price
- Quality Relations
- Servitization

Decision-Making   Collaboration

Business Performance

Expansion   Profit

Design To Market

Control
- Governance
- Public Policy
- Leadership

Cocreation
- Products
- Services
- Values

Market Attributes and Competition

Bottom Line
- New product Development
- Design and Systems Thinking
- Industrial Marketing
- Engineering Reverse Innovations
- Localization vs Globalization
- Ambidexterity in Business modeling

Dynamics
- Market
- Information
- Economy

- Taxonomy of Markets
- Types of Demand
- Supply-chain management
- Retailing infrastructure
- Nature and Type of Competition
- Branding and Promotion
- Consumption Pattern
- Shared Values Management

Measures
- Strategy
- Implementation
- Evaluation

Figure 2.1 Attributes of design-to-market strategy ecosystem

Source: Author

to enhance their outreach to customers and increase the effectiveness to design-to-market strategies. The success of design-to-market strategies depends on leadership styles (transformational and transactional) and bottom-up governance practices (feedback-driven strategy development, reverse accountability, and value chain management). The functional impetus in managing design-to-market strategies is evidenced in the firms by adapting to the following strategies:

- Continuous innovation (incremental and ambidextrous innovations)
- Technology deployment (cost, time, risk, and lifecycle)
- Resources management (crowdfunding, collective governance, public funding, and institutional debt)
- Differentiation (design attributes, unique selling proposition, and key differentiators)
- Cost–price–quality relationship (affordability, adaptability, quality assurance, and segmented pricing)
- Servitization (embedded product and customers services on purchases)

Most firms with a successful implementation of design-to-market policies tend to map market attributes and analyze competition ecosystem to deploy effective marketing strategies. The business strategies vary by types of market and demand as discussed as follows:

- Existing markets with high demand for products, lead to high competition and low market share, and generate low profitability. Though such market situation is attractive to the firms, the prospect of business growth is very slow due to marginalization of market share, high rate of customer defections, and low-price competitions.
- Potential markets with latent demand drive firms to explore near monopolistic market advantage. Such market situation provides the firms the opportunity to become market leaders and maintain the lead by acquiring higher number of customer than the firms competing in the

similar segments. The near monopolistic market situation offers scope to generate high loyalty among customer and profit over time.

- Dormant markets require customers to be educated on new products and services and create demand. Most firms engaged in new product development face the challenge of creating demand and invest resources in customer education programs. Firms in such product demand and market situation over time enjoy the benefits of near monopoly and lead the market by building customer loyalty.

In addition, market attributes that support design-to-market attributes include supply chain management, technology-led retailing infrastructure (by developing self-help kiosks, augmented reality, radiofrequency-based identification (RFID), and visual merchandizing tools), branding and promotion, and managing shared values. Customer-centric firms tend to develop social interface of their business to understand customers' problems, needs, and expected solutions to improve social value and lifestyle. These firms have more effective corporate social responsibility programs than other firms operating in the industrial marketing segments. Consequently, social marketing has emerged as a stronger value-creating strategy as compared to any other competitive marketing strategy. The bottom line of the design-to-marketing strategy envelops the challenges of new product development, integrating systems thinking, managing reverse innovations, ambidexterity, and developing synergy with global and local business models. The design-to-market canvas has four facets comprising organizational strategies (constituting design, resources, philosophy, and culture), key functionaries (business partners, employees, and stakeholders), measures (strategy, implementation, and evaluation), and dynamics (the attribute of markets, information analysis, and economic factors as illustrated in Figure 2.1.

Companies find the design-to-market strategies challenging. Nonetheless, most customer-centric companies are engaged in co-creating marketing strategies by examining strengths and weaknesses through customers and stakeholders. The major task for companies in implementing design-to-market strategies are to outmaneuver the disruptive and low-cost competitors. Successful price competitors, such as the German retailer Aldi, and an American pharmaceutical-cum-convenience stores CVS, are altering competition by employing several tactics such as narrowing down the customer segments, delivering value through the basic product, and supporting low prices with cost-efficient business operations. Managing market competition by focusing on the non-price factors such as technology, quality of products, servitization, social and individual values, and co-creation have emerged in the 21st century corporate philosophy to lead the market. However, ignoring cut-price rivals may eventually force companies to desert all market segments over time. Certainly, the price wars by slashing prices is not a strategic solution for companies aiming at leading the market. Usually, lower profits for incumbents is caused due to the low-cost entrants in the business. Companies tend to take defensive approaches in competing against low price–low strategic vision companies in certain circumstances (Kumar 2006).

The design-to-market strategies are evolved around various elements of marketing mix, which enhance the market competitiveness of firms. The key attributes of marketing mix including innovation and technology are able to effectively manage the marketing performance, customer values, and competitive growth synergy in a business organization. These elements have extensive effects among all the interrelated business operations of the firm. Therefore, creating holistic customer experience and marketing experience by implementing the marketing-mix strategies has been the priority of many customer-centric companies. Implementation of effective marketing strategy is a "building block" exercise, which requires perfect coordination among various elements of marketing mix and associated attributes like emotions, validity of decisions, and customer value. However, marketing-mix practices can be modified in reference to the culture, strategy formation process, market-focused strategic organizational behaviors, and marketing control systems of the marketing organization (Slater et al. 2010). Brands are positioned in the competitive marketplace using the attributes of marketing-mix elements. A price–benefit positioning map helps firms explore customer perceptions on comparison of products in a competitive marketplace. The brand value structure also unites the customer's sensory, emotional, social, and intellectual experiences in a positive way within the contemporary business environment (Tsai 2005). Firms are leaning toward developing the hybrid marketing mix following the advancement of innovation and technology and transforming traditional marketing approaches using the digital technologies to enhance customer values, market competitiveness, and profitability.

Successful companies are selective toward systematically developing strategies to create and lead new markets. Customer-centric companies develop marketing strategies using the marketing-mix elements appropriately designed for acquiring new customers and retaining those existing by providing competitive leverage and customer value. Developing marketing strategies for new customers with unfamiliar brands is challenging for the companies. An appropriate marketing mix also guides companies in minimizing cost–time–risk convergence in marketing and optimizing market share and profitability. The marketing-mix concept has been tested long before by the companies and has become the base of marketing theory. Marketing strategies based on the basic elements such as product, price, place, and promotion are effective and simple to implement. However, consistency in strategy implementation, integration of marketing-mix elements, and systematically exploiting the competitive leverage make managers see how a marketing program fits the needs of the customers and marketplace. The integrated map of hybrid marketing-mix elements is presented in Table 2.1.

Besides the 11Ps, the peripheral marketing mix constitutes quadruple elements of As, Vs, Cs, and Es that help the firms in acquiring higher precision in the developing marketing strategies than working with the conventional wisdom as illustrated in Table 2.1. In addition, there are several points of convergence among marketing-mix elements, which highlight the integrated effect of marketing strategies and their performance in the competitive marketplace. The hybrid marketing mix is a combination of co-created marketing strategies and management of innovation and technology as strategy drivers as illustrated in Table 2.1. The hybrid marketing is founded on the taxonomy of innovations

Table 2.1 *Hybrid marketing mix*

Core Marketing-Mix Elements				
Hybrid Foundation		**Advanced Marketing Mix**		
Innovation	Technology	Basic Elements	Functional Elements	Corporate Element
Frugal innovation	Digital technology	Product	Packaging (Technology)	Posture (Reputation)
Incremental innovation	Robotic technology	Price	Pace (Time and Space)	Proliferation (Expansion)
Reverse innovation	Self-service technology	Place	People (Frontliners)	
Social innovations	Intermediate technology	Promotion	Performance (Profitability)	
Eco-innovations	Transactional technology		Psychodynamics	

Hybrid Management

- Knowledge diffusion and Transfer of technology
- Managerial skills and Digitization of commerce
- Customer acquaintance and ease of technology use
- Technology lifecycle, investment, and disruptions
- Innovations, accountability, and value creation
- Collective intelligence and social media effects
- Co-creation, coevolution, co-governance
- Stakeholder and customers responsiveness
- Coopetition philosophy and strategic alliances
- Segmentation, targeting, and digital branding
- Artificial intelligence and augmented reality

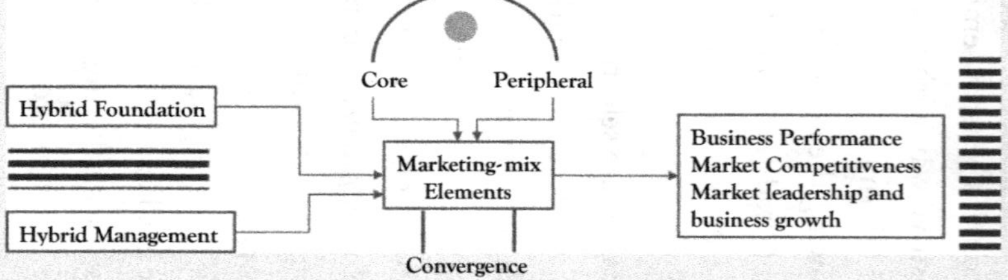

Figure: T2.1 Operational Flow of Hybrid Marketing Mix

Source: Author

Peripheral Marketing-mix Elements				
Convergence	4As	4Vs	4Cs	4Es
AATAR	Awareness	Validity	Cost to customer	Exploring
ACCA	Attributes	Value	Convenience	Enhancement
VRINE	Affordability	Venue	Communication	Emotions
PIRT	Adaptability	Vogue	Conflicts	Experience

Abbreviations: AATAR, Awareness, Attributes, Trial, Availability, Repeat buying; ACCA, Awareness, Comprehension, Conviction, Action; VRINE, Value, Rarity, Inimitability, Nonsubstitutability, Exploitability; PIRT, Personality, Image, Responsiveness, Trust.

Source: Author

(frugal, incremental, reverse, social, and ecological) and technology dynamics. The growing technologies that affect the marketing strategies include digital (e-commerce), robotic (industrial and domestic appliances), self-service technologies (automatic teller machine and vending machines), intermediate technologies (home-grown and low-cost technologies), and transactional technologies (RFID technology, Block-Chain logistics and inventory technologies, and augmented reality technology in retailing). Managing hybrid marketing strategies requires diffusion of knowledge and technology, which would not only inculcate interest in customers toward technology-driven products but also improve the skills among retailers. The underlying challenge in promoting e-commerce is to familiarize online and store technologies with the customers. The collective intelligence and social media effects drive co-creation of innovative products. Social and customer-oriented technologies coevolve within the social business ecosystem and encourage co-governance of innovation and technology products. Table 2.1 demonstrates that firms make investment in innovation and technology by meticulously evaluating the expected returns. However, there remains the task of managing products and services against the technology disruptions and value creation among customers in rapidly changing market scenarios. The inset Figure T2.1 exhibits the flow of hybrid marketing mix leading to business performance, market competitiveness, and market leadership and business growth. To improve the business performance and growth of the company within the vagaries of the competition, the elements of the marketing mix contributes effectively to the strengths and protect from competitive threats. However, analysis of marketing-mix elements also guides managers to overcome the internal weaknesses and explore right opportunities (Shapiro 1985). The increasing challenge for the companies is to develop marketing strategy for identical products as compared to the similar products with differentiation. Companies bottling purified water face the challenge of marketing it in the identical product segment. The brand needs a strong unique selling proposition to lead the market by increasing its market share. The Harmonie Mineral Water, the second best-selling bottled water in the world, has developed marketing strategies using the attributes of marketing-mix elements (11 Ps) as discussed as follows:

- Product (attributes, process technology, unique propositions)
- Price (pricing based on brand taxonomy-classic, go to, and gallon brands)
- Place (360° distribution in the service areas)
- Promotion (periodical and competitive customer promotions)
- Packaging (ergonomic, by volume, convenience, recyclable and bisphenol A (bpa) free)
- Pace (first-mover advantage in selected markets, market challenger)
- People (sales and customer services)
- Performance (quality, services, technology, and value creation)
- Psychodynamics (social networking of customers, experience sharing, shared value propositions)
- Posture (corporate image, and brand equity)
- Proliferation (market expansion)

Companies can draw a strategy map based on selected marketing-mix elements, in the context of specific market scenarios to manage products and services in competitive markets. Such a strategy mapping helps managers conduct less expensive and time-consuming market surveys against the shortcomings of those competing. Creating a strategy map to adapt the design-to-market goals involves the following steps:

- Defining target customers and market, and holistically viewing the market to include all products that customers might consider against the existing substitutes
- Tracking customer preferences, use values, preferred price, promotions, and peer reviews that motivate buying behavior
- Identifying preferred take-away behavior of customers such as wholesale, retail or bundled products and services
- Identifying primary benefit of products in the context of innovation, technology, use value, lifecycle, and value for money. This explains most of the variance in the product preferences and pricing effects, and
- Mapping product position approaches against the competing products in a given market by plotting the effects of customer buying behavior due to the elements of marketing mix.

Such a strategy map would get a picture of the competitive landscape of marketplace, which would educate managers to pick up the right marketing strategy with the combination of elements of marketing mix. The strategy maps with design-to-market goals of Harley-Davidson motorcycles, Samsung mobile phones, and the leisure services companies like J. W. Marriott and Hilton helped the firms locate potential markets for their products and services and identify new opportunities for expanding business. These maps also allowed companies to anticipate and develop timely counterstrategies to outperform the competing products and services (e.g., D'Aveni 2007).

Consumer Behavior and Design Strategy

Customer needs are changing continuously as the innovation and technology grow at a rapid pace. Consequently, no uniform marketing strategy fits into a market. Customer-centric companies develop marketing strategies specific to products and markets by evaluating the strengths and weaknesses of competing products. The design-to-market goals are co-created by the firms in association with the customers, promoters, suppliers, and retailers. Successful marketing strategies reduce the customer stress and increase purchase intentions. In the dynamic markets with high competition, innovative products and services, and changing preferences, customers often experience behavioral dilemma. The consumer behavior can be altered through social influence, sales motivations, and other psychosocial factors (Tsai 2019). The customer preferences are also driven by the social and ethnic influences, self-image congruence, and anthropomorphic perceptions. For example, the Barbie doll was one of the most iconic toys representing cultural and ethnic values since long. However, the industry landscape and customer preferences are changing to adapt to the fashion trends. Barbie has been in the spotlight in developing countries as customers have criticized the doll for providing a narrow and unrealistic vision of women and the sense of dressing (Robson and Beninger 2016).

As customer preferences are changing rapidly, companies are developing design-thinking strategies considering the competitive leverage over time. Such approach illustrates the classical first-mover advantage to drive the customer loyalty and competitive advantage on the products and services. In the fast-growing markets driven by innovations and information technology, time has become the principal source of competitive advantage. Companies tend to reach customers and offer them competitive benefits through co-created organization practices and design. Companies shorten the time of operations and provide customers with better products and services, and lower costs to remain competitive. The market cycle of the customer-centric products comprises incubation time (in company production), supply-chain activities (backward and forward linkages), display and sales speed (in store, online, and promotions), customer relations (value co-creation, social marketing, and psychodynamics), and competitive lead (overriding challengers and achieving high brand equity). Customer-centric companies therefore organize product-market teams around small, autonomous, multifunctional managers. The product positioning and delivery system are affected by the temporal and spatial dimensions, which construct learning loops for the firms toward sharing knowledge and experience among customers (Bower and Hout 1988).

Customer products companies are at the edge of co-creating products today by commercialization of local innovations for wider markets. Godrej (India), General Electric (USA), Nestle (Europe), and Unilever (UK) have successfully experimented blending the local–global innovations, which may be identified as reverse innovation, to set their business roots in local markets. The emerging corporate innovation model today is globally collaborative in reference to new product ideas, customer insights, business resources, and entrepreneurial intelligence coming from all over. For instance, more than 50 percent of innovation initiatives of Proctor & Gamble involve collaboration with outsiders. Innovations in the global marketplace have evolved from customer needs to futuristic solutions. Local companies customize products and services to meet ethnic customer needs and slowly follow the economies of scale. Small emerging companies develop business models to overcome market-specific difficulties and attempt to gain competitive advantage against the multinational brands in the marketplace over time. However, customers prefer to stay with the companies, who deliver products and services with the latest technologies and augment competitive advantage. Regional companies gain price leadership quickly as they find ways to support low price strategy through the low-cost labor and offering in-house training to their employees in lieu of hiring skilled employees, which escalate costs. Successful homegrown champions that have grown global include a few multinationals such as Yum Brands, Nokia, and Hyundai. They have managed to overturn the local competitors by using the aforementioned organizational and marketing management strategies (Bhattacharya and Michael 2008).

The evolution of markets over the centuries has been a perennial phenomenon congruent with the shifts in social, economic, and technological knowledge in the society. The evolution of business and growth has promoted economic behavior to explore the markets. Sociologically the evolution of markets was based on the understanding that individuals are embedded in various cognitive structures involving the business activities. Shifts in the market processes in the society are induced by fundamental beliefs and shared assumptions, and resemble elements of social culture defining norms of markets, expected behavior, and thought. Such business evolution paradigms are resistant to minor discrepancies between their fundamental models and contradicting (potentially empirical) evidence. Thus, discrepancies in market behavior are considered as socioeconomic abnormalities, paradoxes or puzzles in a given place and time (Hedaa and Ritter 2005; Rajagopal 2012).

Upon understanding how markets have evolved over the years around the customers' problems, needs, and solutions, companies need to manage the more complex grid of emotions, personality, social influence, and self-image congruence. The benefits to companies can be huge, if they conduct research to explore psychoanalytical and neurocentral behavioral elements affecting customer behavior. Most firms know their customers sketchily, and the marketing strategies are based on their innate assumption, competitive response, and rapid guesswork rather than scientific analysis of customer insights and strategic requirements. Consequently, the companies, who back their marketing strategies, are more successful than those, who play "guess and goal" game to gain competitive advantage. Analyzing the existing market research and customer insight data and understanding the qualitative descriptions better than the quantitative results of behavioral dimensions can benefit the customer-centric companies. The psychosocial desires for boosting superiority, economic freedom, security, and success are the hidden indicators, which need to be unveiled by the companies to not only boost customer satisfaction, but also achieve competitive leverage in the marketplace. Successful customer-centric companies encourage customers with high loyalty, proactiveness, and motivation on social media and rewards them to serve as effective referrals for the company to market their brands. These customers serve as important collective knowledge agents to the mass and premier customer segments. Therefore, connecting to emotions help companies acquire new customers and retain the most valuable customer segment. Food products, fashion, cosmetics, apparel, and customer electronics products companies make the organization's commitment to emotional connection as a key indicator for their competitive growth (Magids et al. 2015).

Customer culture existing in the society, and the language appeal of communications also affect the customer perceptions, attitudes, and consumption behavior. Material culture affects the level of demand, the quality and types of products demanded, and their functional features, as well as the means of production of these goods and their distribution. Material culture includes the tools and artifacts, the material or physical things in a society, excluding the physical things found in nature unless they undergo some technological procedure. Language determines the brand etymology. It is an important cultural tool for developing consumer behavior. Brand names in reference to linguistic assets such as phonetics (sounds), etymology (roots of words) and rhetoric (persuasive discourse) enhance the customer awareness and knowledge and develop customer perceptions. The quality of translation of brand communication from the original source also affects the customer perception and psychodynamics of customers. Social institutions play a significant role in nurturing the cultural heritage, which is reflected in the individual behavior. Such institutions include family, education, and political structures. The media affects the ways in which people relate to one another, organize their activities to live in harmony with one another, teach acceptable behavior to succeeding generations, and govern themselves. The status of gender in society, the family, social classes, group behavior, age groups; and how societies define decency and civility are interpreted differently within every culture. Social institutions are a system of regulatory norms and rules of governing actions in pursuit of immediate ends in terms of their conformity with the ultimate common value system of a community (Rajagopal 2019).

Availability of new products in market not only allures but also forces the customers to change their consumption behavior at a hidden psychological cost and economic pressure. Many products face the risk of customers and promoters irrationally overvaluing the benefits of the new products, which drives the companies to overvalue their own innovations than the felt reality. Nonetheless, such conflicts can be averted in business, and the disconnected strategies can be redesigned by improving and encouraging easy selling products, minimizing the foreseen failures, long product lifecycle, and stimulating quick response of customers to the innovative products. The market scenarios vary by products and the behavior of customers. Markets have different ratios of product improvement to alter customer preferences by redefining the product solutions. Companies that are able to fix their market–product variabilities into the consumer behavior grid, can prepare customers for the innovative product and reform their apprehensions on the products, benefits, and marketing strategies (Gourville 2006).

Consumer behavior is growing complex with the advancement of frugal and disruptive innovations, and affordable technologies such as social, domestic, and light industrial robots that influence customers. The rapid and abrupt shifts in consumer behavior has thrown major challenges of achieving market competitiveness and consistent lead to the customer-centric companies. Therefore, the design thinking has become a popular tool to develop customer-centric marketing strategies. The design-to-market strategies have helped companies co-create products for customers with high perceived use value. IKEA home décor, furniture, and fixtures based on the need and design suggested by the customers, Lego Creation from static models to power driven creations, and simplified Oral-B electric toothbrush from P&G, which has reduced from many functions to two for customer convenience, set the right examples of the use of design thinking to induce consumer behavior. Conventionally, design has been a downstream perspective in the product development process for the high-value customer segment. Over time, with the convergence of collective intelligence and customer research, firms have focused on developing new products with perceived aesthetics, and inculcating brand perception among customers. The digital and reminiscent advertising of products have helped firms in making customers understand about the design attributes in products and perceive values. Consequently, the design thinking has gone public today and is known for its contributions in marketing with customers. The design and innovation encompass collective intelligence today that exhibits not only the customer demand but also emotions associated with the products and buying decisions. The emotions and personality of customers associated with the products are evolved around the creative ideas, product attributes, complementarity, and user-oriented designs. These factors significantly contribute to the design-to-market concepts of developing and managing new products rather than simply managing them with a conventional marketing strategy. Design thinking has emerged as a method to deliver needs and desires of customers through streamlined solutions, which could attain high market share. The design process is carried out in a technologically feasible and strategically viable (cost-time-risk-profit) manner. The most challenging situation in the design-thinking process is the radical change in cost–time–risk factors combined with customer brainstorming and rapid prototyping. Most design-to-market products are developed using innovative processes and software that radically streamline information exchange between the companies, stakeholders, and key partners (Brown 2008). The strategy wheel connecting the design thinking and consumer behavior is exhibited in Figure 2.2.

The strategy wheel illustrated in the Figure 2.2 is metaphorical to the gyroscopic effect in the bicycle wheel. A rotating bicycle wheel has angular momentum, which is a property involving the speed of rotation (market competition), the mass of the wheel (corporate business), and how the mass is distributed (customer orientation). The angular momentum (market coverage) is characterized by both size (global, regional, domestic, and niche markets) and direction (strategic vs tactical market behavior) The strategy wheel presented in Figure 2.2 has customer domain (large wheel) and the market domain (small wheel) comprising the competitive pressure built in the market and the up-thrust corporate response to the pressure respectively. In this scenario, the gyroscopic effect can be explained as follows: due to the pressure of market competition, companies tend to implement strategic and tactical changes (rotation of

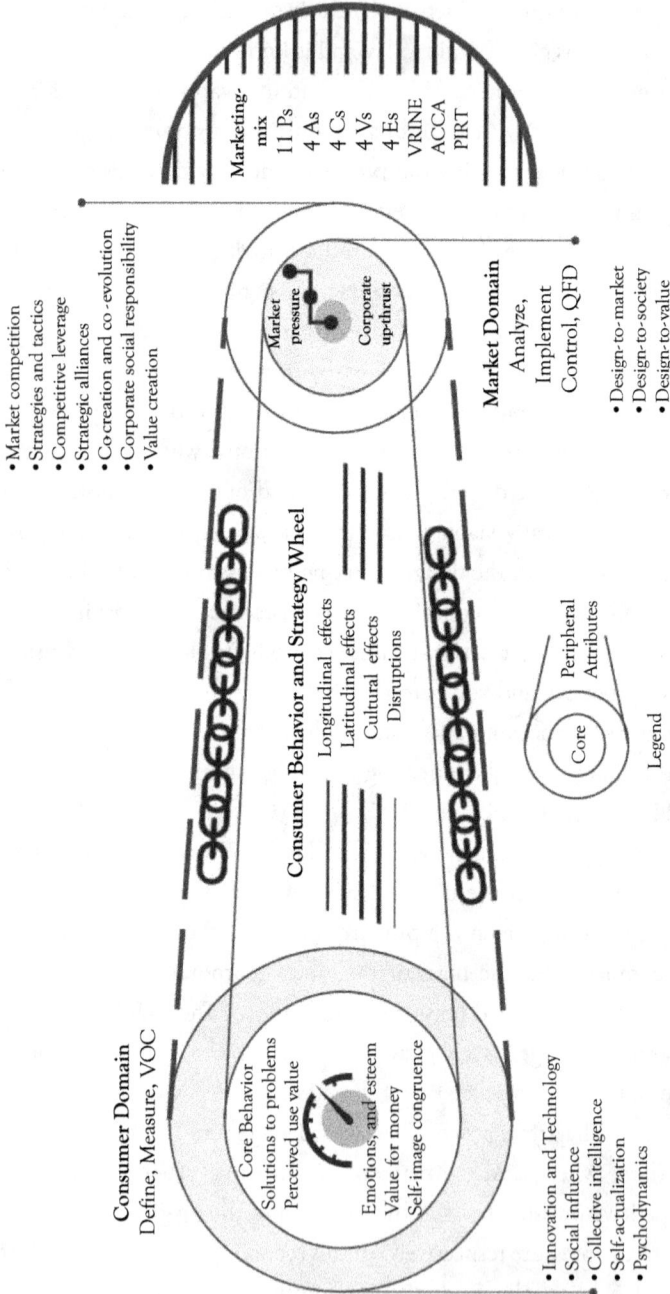

Consumer Domain
Define, Measure, VOC

• Market competition
• Strategies and tactics
• Competitive leverage
• Strategic alliances
• Cocreation and co-evolution
• Corporate social responsibility
• Value creation

Marketing-
mix
11 Ps
4 As
4 Cs
4 Vs
4 Es
VRINE
ACCA
PIRT

Market Domain
Analyze,
Implement
Control, QFD

• Design-to-market
• Design-to-society
• Design-to-value

Market
pressure

Corporate
up-thrust

Consumer Behavior and Strategy Wheel
Longitudinal effects
Latitudinal effects
Cultural effects
Disruptions

Peripheral
Attributes

Core

Legend

Core Behavior
Solutions to problems
Perceived use value

Emotions, and esteem
Value for money
Self-image congruence

• Innovation and Technology
• Social influence
• Collective intelligence
• Self-actualization
• Psychodynamics

Figure 2.2 Consumer behavior and strategy wheel

Source: Author.

small wheel), which drive the major changes in customer preferences, perceptions, attitude, and behavior (impact on large wheel). The critical performance factors associated with the customer domain that companies need to learn include: defining the need by analyzing the customer solution to the problems, measuring the economic and personal benefits, and acting on the voice of customers. The market domain encourages companies to analyze competitive trends, implement counter or cooperative strategies to align with the market competition, and deploy controls in managing the cost, price, operations, supply chain management and services deliveries to customers and key business partners. The metaphorical gyro principal to market design illustrates that corporate up-thrust in the market domain drives longitudinal (over time) and latitudinal (territorial) effects in reconstructing consumer behavior toward psycho-neurotic elements (emotions, self-esteem, self-image congruence, and values) besides extrinsic behavioral factors. The external influences that tend to moderate the consumer behavior include the growing benefits of innovations and technology, socio-cultural shifts, inflow of information and collective intelligence, and psychodynamics driven by the face-to-face and digital interactions. These factors significantly influence the consumer behavior and the process of self-actualization within the socioeconomic ecosystem. The market domain drives companies to derive impetus on developing competitive strategies and building corporate posture within the industry. Accordingly, firms tend to develop strategies under the following business philosophies:

Design-to-market:	Strategies related to business-to-customers, business-to-business, services, target segments, competitiveness, and profitability
Design-to-society:	Strategies to gain social value through co-creation, coevolution, corporate social responsibilities, and corporate involvement in social innovations
Design-to-value:	Develop customer-centric strategies to enhance perception, attitude, and behavioral perspectives. Design-to-value strategies are focused toward co-creating customer values, building self-esteem, and loyalty.

The corporate up-thrust is directed toward developing competitive marketing strategies and tactics to gain leverage in the marketplace by forming strategic alliances with the key business partners. Marketplace of the 21st century has shifted from conventional philosophy of over-riding the competitors to focusing on business continuum through co-creation and coevolution along with the business partners. Such business models help in integrating competition spread in the market and building a consortium. The for-profit consortiums include Airbus Industrie GIE, composed of the companies British Aerospace, Aérospatiale, Construcciones Aeronáuticas SA. Similarly, Hulu, composed of Comcast, Time Warner, the Walt Disney Company, and 21st Century Fox can be cited as a business consortium. Among many business consortiums, the airline manufacturer Airbus Industrie GIE is a profitable one. European aerospace manufacturers collaborate within the consortium to produce and sell commercial aircrafts. In the customer products segment, the dairy industry in India led by the regional dairy cooperatives under a single umbrella organization—Anand Milk Union Limited (AMUL) is a successful for-profit cooperative consortium. The design strategies are supported by following the core and auxiliary elements of marketing mix (see Figure 2.2) in addition to the synergizing elements affecting the marketing strategies are explained in Table 2.1.

The elements of marketing mix have evolved over the years in reference to the changing business environment, shifts in industry focus, and government regulations. The fundamental elements of marketing mix comprising product, price, place, and promotion still dominate the process of developing the marketing strategy. Most successful companies like General Electric, Procter and Gamble, and Cisco believed in developing customer-centric marketing mix to enhance market performance of the products and services. An effective marketing mix actively pushes the innovative and unfamiliar brands in the market by making clear passages through the competition to serve the target markets. However, customer-centric companies need the coordination of strategies across several elements of marketing mix to develop an effective marketing-mix canvas, and link the strategy implementation to business performance metrics such as product, price, place, and sales (Dawar and Bagga 2015).

Co-creation and Collective Intelligence

Consulting the customers and stakeholders in the process of designing products and marketing strategies has emerged as a prominent tool in the contemporary businesses. Co-creation is an ideation process in developing new products with the experience, emotions, and engagement of customers. Digital interface of companies with customers and stakeholders, and mass interactions on social media channels have enabled companies to leverage the co-creation process in the era of Internet of Things. Customer-centric businesses derive in-depth insights into what, how, and with whom customers want to interact during the co-creation process. It is all about learning customer experiences and documenting their expectations on various dimensions of product and process design, and the designing the marketing strategies. Customer information can be analyzed in several ways of participation including motives, design ideas, challenges, intrinsic interests, and radical thought, which help companies in developing their design framework. The co-creation perceptual map explains different ideas and customer expectations over time and space. However, there remains ambiguity and duplication in customer perceptions across the informational channels as personal characteristics and expectations toward virtual co-creation (Fuller 2010). In implementing co-created strategies, companies use the traditional structure of the Balanced Scorecard, and engage stakeholders to gain dramatic shifts in the business performance.

Companies have managed to develop marketing strategies and their performance with conventional wisdom by collecting and analyzing opinion on marketing from customers, supply chain operators, vendors, and employees. However, the traditional process has been ambiguous for the companies to integrate the voice of customers in strategy development. Such processes focus on repeatability and compliance and lead to stagnation. The diverse growth of interactive digital communities has led the companies to explore possibilities of seeking new ideas from the stakeholders and coevolve business models over time in the competitive marketplace. With the advancement of information technology, co-creation has emerged as a better approach to collectively solve problems and exploit opportunities. It allows firms to continually acquire skills and insights of stakeholders, and plan to develop new designs in products, services, and strategies to generate value for all. The co-creation process is planned on both physical and digital platforms to explore new experiences and connections, and grow organically (Gouillart and Billings 2013).

Advances in digital technologies have augmented the scope of outsourcing the business activities beyond geographic boundaries through several independent contributors. Crowdsourcing is a creative tool used by companies today to expand their outreach to customers, map their perceptions, and understand their behavioral implications in business. Overtime, this tool has led to collective intelligence, which helps the companies build the *design cube,* integrating design-to-market, design-to-society, and design-to-value dimensions in business modeling process. The analysis of collective intelligence helps the firms not only in exploring new business opportunities but also in commercializing reverse innovations that have significant market potential. Commercializing the crowdsourced ideas is often a disruptive leap to hit competing products in the target market. The collective insights help in developing co-created business models to drive an impact in the emerging market through popular attributes of products, pricing, promotions, packaging, and managing customer psychodynamics based on collectively generated contents. In fact, crowdsourcing has led to the emergence of some entirely new business models. Such crowd-based business models (CBBMs) can lead to an important competitive advantage, simultaneously presenting new challenges to entrepreneurs and executives. The collective intelligence process is a decision driver, which grows organically in the organization as a system over time.

Companies have been practicing team approach to identify customer needs and solve problems. The focus group discussions have helped the customer-centric companies explore customer needs, while customer surveys prove to be instrumental in knowing the market from customers' perspectives. However, in applied context, identifying right needs, developing solutions, exploring opportunities, and understanding the behavioral complexities are challenging for companies, and are often founded on the wrong assumptions. Many contemporary Web applications provide access to the collective segment on a greater scale than ever before.

Indeed, the increasing use of information markets, wikis, crowdsourcing, social networks, collaborative software, and other web-based tools constitutes a paradigm shift to "wisdom of crowds" concept to develop decision models in business. However, the sporadic growth of the blogs and the proliferation of social interactive platforms necessitate a framework to screen the ingenuity of such sources that generate collective knowledge for use in business decision making. Google has been benefited by the collective intelligence in making successful business decisions by implementing the inflow controls on collective contents, preserving diversity, stakeholder engagement, and intellectual property management through digital rights (Bonabeau 2009).

Conceptually, collective intelligence encourages a pro-customer and pro-society business modeling that helps businesses grow within the social ecosystem. However, determining the collective value to the firm and capturing value effectively from mass information pose major challenges in developing the CBBMs. Building corporate goals and strategies on the crowd capital perspective, and developing tactics and practices on the crowdsourced ideas, often turns chaotic. In designing innovative CBBMs for their industries, decision making get inspired by the appropriately filtered collective ideas in the context of social innovation, competitive advantage, technological feasibility, and economic viability (Tauscher 2017). Contemporary marketing has evolved alongside the customer-centric perspectives as a cognitive science and has spanned across advanced marketing mix comprising core and peripheral elements (see Table 2.1). Therefore, customer value has become central to business modeling. Most companies develop marketing strategies (a principal constituent of business model) on assumptions of customer values, which might misfit while implementing a business model. Collective intelligence provides the real perceptions of customers and the rationale for new products and services. Advancement of information technology has enabled crowdsourcing practices among innovation-oriented companies. Crowdsourced information is obtained through a designated website or through text mining. The designated call centers today are also capable of collecting crowdsourced data through an open call to the masses via the Internet. Crowdsourcing is a process supported by information technology that has enabled organizations to collect and manage temporal and spatial information. In the recent past, research and practice on crowdsourcing have continued to grow, evolve, and revolutionize the development of collaborative business models. Although numerous studies have been conducted in this area, it appears that the main components involved in the crowdsourcing processes remain limited (Modaresnezhad et al. 2020). The integrated business models with stakeholders' commitment can be explained in terms of their value proposition, and value creation and delivery though effective corporate social responsibility. These perspectives need to be discussed in terms of public information, consumption, and managing constituents of collective business ecosystems through global–local interactive information exchange. Though the literature proposes several conceptual solutions, there is a need to rethink on modular designs and co-creation of business models within global–local business dynamics (Bridgens et al. 2017).

New Product Development

Innovation of new products is a complex process that needs to be carried out meticulously in the firms integrating the business and customer use values in the marketplace. Firms engaged in innovating products should map customers' needs, attributes of close substitutes, competitive threats, required product services, and estimated cost of marketing of the product in different markets. However, the rate of failure of innovative services is higher as compared to the customer products. These products largely include credit cards, insurance schemes, hire purchase schemes, investment plans, and the like. Most companies consider the process of innovative product development as colossal due to the cumbersome stage gate process of manufacturing, and organizational and market led intricacies in analyzing key indicators to launch and manage the products in the competitive marketplace. However, the process of developing an innovative product can be made easier by rationally dividing the chronology of the process into two parts: an early stage, which focuses on evaluating prospects and eliminating bad bets; and a late stage that optimizes the market potential. Eli Lilly, following this approach, designed and piloted Chorus, an autonomous unit dedicated solely to the early stage. Chorus has significantly improved efficiency of new product development and productivity at Lilly. Although the unit absorbs just one-tenth of Lilly's investment in the early-stage development, it delivers a substantially greater fraction of the molecules slated for late second phase trials at almost twice the speed and less than a third of the cost of the standard process, sometimes saving as much as two years from the usual development time (Bonabeau et al. 2008).

The product and business strategies of a foreign firm should be developed in reference to the macroeconomic conditions of the host country. The definition of the product objectives should emerge from the business definitions developed in accordance with the macroeconomic requirements of the host country. The foreign firms need to analyze whether the success of their product or product line can be replicated in a new market destination abroad and explore the factors that may lead them to the market leadership. In other words, a decision must be made to select the more appropriate product design strategy considering standardization or customization. *Standardization* refers to offering a uniform product on a national, regional, or worldwide basis, while *customization* signifies adapting a product, making appropriate changes in it, to match local perspectives. A firm may decide for product customization according to the size of the market and the competitive advantage in the long run. The customization of the product may be chosen over standardization to cater to the unique situation in each country. Yet, there are potential gains to be considered in product standardization. International marketers must examine all the criteria in order to decide the extent to which products should vary from country to country (Aaker and Joachimsthaler 1999). If there are no new needs to be catered to make the product offering ready for any market, resulting in a significant cost saving, the firm may decide to standardize its products. However, product standardization may turn a risky proposition in the long run due to the switching consumer behavior that tends to change over time. However, some international companies have succeeded in standardization of products for offering them in many countries. The General Electric Company's debacles in the small-appliances field in Germany, and Polaroid's difficulties with the Swinger camera in France are the classic examples of product standardization. Contrary to this, Volkswagen's worldwide success with Beetle (Classic and sports versions) supports standardization.

Idea generation in the process of new product development is a major exercise. This technique calls for listing all major attributes of the existing product and the needed attributes in order to improve the same product. The forced relationship of the new product with the existing accessories also needs to be studied, for example, developing a new television set may be related with the customer need of clock, multichannel viewing on one screen, microphone attachment, and a built-in video game. Such forced relationship has to be identified by the company before launching the product. The morphological analysis calls for identifying the structural dimensions of a problem and examining the relationships among them. The need identification can be done by interacting with the potential and existing customers in a focus group meet (Rajagopal 2015).

Front-end activities comprising concept development, concept–design alignment, and concept commercialization allow customer-centric firms to validate strategies accordingly. The combination and synchronization of these elements largely influence the process and performance of new product development. Firms create new ideas through any means such as the internal ideation process, crowdsourcing, or hybrid insights comprising internal ideation, collective intelligence, and aligned technology design. Such a systematic approach provides the firms not only the design-thinking perspectives for products but also enables them to develop design-to-market strategies, which gives the firms directions to gain competitive leverage, enhance customer outreach, and product dynamics in the marketplace (Floren and Frishammar 2012).

New product development and marketing cycle are also affected by the innovation diffusion cycle spread across the same stages as of product innovation cycle. In the introduction cycle, the diffusion of information is often low as firms do not put adequate resources in generating awareness on the innovation. Firms invite lead users in this stage to test the innovated product and influence early adopters on the usage of product. Lead users form a small group but act as powerful referrals and brand carriers. Firms spend adequate resources in the growth stage to diffuse product innovation attributes through direct communication on one-on-one basis to drive intensive effect on the innovation-led products among early adopters. Customers in this group are strong followers of the lead users and stand as effective opinion leaders for influencing the early majority of customers. Most companies deploy enormous resources in advertising, communication, and social media involvement during the late growth and maturity stage to drive customers who are less affluent, less educated, but ready to experiment the innovative products. The "early majority" customer segment constitutes a relatively larger segment than the previous customer segments, but it is confined to niche. However, the following stage is of late majority, which is a very large segment and often represents about half of the total number of customers in a given market area. This customer segment exhibits high adaptability with the innovative products and derives satisfactory value-for-money that makes the late majority customers frequent buyers. Customers in this segment are price sensitive and pose the threat of defection when more attractive substitute products penetrate in the market. However, a small number of customers in each market segment are hard to drive for buying any innovative product as they are indecisive and difficult to convince. Such segment of customers is found in all stages of growth of innovative products but is apparently huge in number during the decline stage of the product lifecycle.

Most emerging companies are keen to benchmark practices on new product development because delivering a new product has a major impact on brand portfolio and performance of the company. Therefore, companies continuously search for best practices that may enable them in carrying out the new product journey efficiently and effectively, from the manufacturing to marketing stages. Companies access best practices through benchmarking studies, Delphi methodology with leading experts, and surveys involving practices of upstream companies. The best practices can be acquired by the firms across the following dimensions:

- Strategy (value-driven and competition oriented across geo-demographic segments)
- Research (periodical customer research to learn customer choices and associated attributes, marketing-mix elements based competitive research, and research on PESTEL factors[1])

---

[1] PESTEL factors include political, economic, social technological, environmental, and legal factors within the market ecosystem that developing strategies and decision making in companies.

- Commercialization (frugal innovation, new products, and social products)
- Process (customization, standardization, simplification, and co-creation)
- Project climate (cost, time, risk, deliverables, and value propositions),
- Company culture (customer-centered, employee-centered, cross-cultural, and leader oriented)
- Metrics/performance measurement (price, profit, market share, growth, and revenue streams).

Such a framework for new product development varies across products and markets alongside the benchmark of best practices. The audit tool is derived from the framework for continuous improvement in the new product across the markets (Barczak and Kahn 2012).

Creativity is associated with the part of the innovation process that is labeled as idea generation. Ideation process for new product development can be stimulated through metaphors, pictures, and experience. It is rooted in the philosophy of rationalism and empiricism, implying "the truth is out there" approaches. It is observed that defining cognitive idea generation is based on personal experiences and beliefs driven by individual and social information. However, these forms of cognitive idea generation process are individualistic and not amenable to team contexts (Bhatt 2000). The basic purpose of this exercise is to generate a large number of ideas. These ideas need to be carefully screened in the interest of customer satisfaction as well as company's profit. In this process, the company should avoid the Drop and Go errors. The former attempts dismiss the good idea, while the latter attempts allow the poor ideas to move into the process of commercialization. Hence, the purpose of screening the idea needs to be understood carefully. It is advised that the company should develop an idea-rating matrix on the basis of the emerging ideas and their usefulness. Product ideas have to be turned into concept, and product concept can be turned later in to a brand concept. The concept testing calls for testing of these competing concepts with an appropriate group of target customers. The concepts can be presented physically or symbolically. The customers' response may be summarized and the strength of the concept may be judged. The need-gap and product-gap levels may be checked and modified thereafter. The concept testing and product development methodology applies to any product or service. Business analysis includes estimating the sales as it would be of one-time purchase, frequently purchased product or at-regular-interval purchased product. Testing new products in markets is a scientific process. Successful test marketing leads to proper uses and also poses serious limitations. It provides a measure of sales performance, and the opportunity to identify and correct any weaknesses in the product or in the marketing plan. It is, however, expensive and arduous. Product development at this stage involves designing the prototypes on the lines of the derived concept that has passed through technical tests.

New product development is not a one-sided effort for companies. Corporate resources, technology, and manufacturing process need to be supported with the effective forward linkages involving suppliers and retailers. Collaboration of suppliers in new product development projects helps in reducing cost, narrowing new product journey time (from conceptualization to manufacturing and marketing), improving quality by considering front-end feedback of suppliers and retailers, and providing scope of implementing retailing technologies that can help augment market share. Supplier integration is successfully driven by large customer-centric companies through a formalized process by managing the supplier capabilities, providing training to suppliers to cope-up with the level of complexity of the technology, and lowering the degree of risk. Leading companies conduct a formal, in-depth supplier evaluation and risk assessment prior to engaging the suppliers in marketing new product marketing (Handfield et al. 1999). Similarly, customer involvement in developing new products has been widely used in American and Japanese manufacturing firms. Quality Function Deployment (QFD) is used as the most popular tool for bringing the voice of the customer into the product development process from conceptual design to manufacturing. The process of QFD begins with a matrix that links customer desires to product engineering requirements, along with competitive benchmarking information, and further matrices can be used to ultimately link this to design of the manufacturing system. Unlike other methods originally developed in the United States and transferred to Japan, the QFD methodology was born out of Total Quality Control (TQC) activities in Japan during the 1960s and has been transferred to companies in the United States. It has been observed that the companies in the United States showed a higher degree of usage, management support, cross-functional involvement, use of QFD-driven data sources, and perceived benefits from using QFD. Customer-involved product development strategies are also found common with the firms in different industries, including Apple, Benetton, Corning, McDonald's, Nike, Nintendo, Sun, and Toyota. The customer firm, often a large original equipment manufacturer, perceives that its power may be cascaded throughout its supply base. At the basic level, cascading is a way for a customer to delegate responsibility to its suppliers. In practice, it has been contended that cascading more often takes the form of a more imposing style of leadership (Lamming et al. 2000).

The launch of product must be carried out in an energetic and creative style with effective promotional package. In planning for the product markets, it is essential to clearly understand the combinations of the expected margins and turnover in volume of the product. Quite often, it is required to operate on volumes rather than looking for the higher margins. This may provide the marketer the opportunity for wide coverage of market at low margins, and helps the firm become the market leader as none of competitors may be able to stand at such low margin due to the problems of reaching economies of scale. It is necessary to position new products in new segments carefully by building image of the brand. The competitive pricing strategy helps in penetrating the product against the competing brands in the new segment. At the same time, it is required to refresh the consumer behavior periodically and reorient brand image in the existing customer segment by building better communication strategies. The success stories of the product help reasonably in carrying out such process.

Customer satisfaction is perceived to be a key driver of long-term relationship between the retailer and the customers, especially when customers are well acquainted with the products and markets, and when industries are highly competitive. Retailing efficiency is one of the principal factors that influence customer satisfaction in a business-to-customer and customer-to-customer context, and help in building customer-retailer dyadic relationship. The key services indicators, which include effective communication, cross-functional teams, and supplier integration, are followed to develop long-term relationships. The customer relationship market is among many different markets a firm needs to consider, with research suggesting that customer retention leads to increased market share and bigger profits. Some practical guidelines have been developed by the customer products companies like IKEA, General Electric Company, Cisco, and Colgate Palmolive on how to design and implement customer relationship management programs. The customer relationship strategies inculcate values that help in building portfolios, and retain the customer and market segments for a long period in order to optimize the profit of the firm.

New products should be launched at appropriate time after getting substantial results from the AATAR applications, which include attributes testing, awareness generation, trial of new product on customers, assuring availability of products, and generating referrals to influence customers toward new products. It has been observed that initially the growth of new products appears weak and slow in the market, and it demands strong organizational support to penetrate in the potential segments. The AATAR applications increase the rate of penetration of new products in the marketplace (Rajagopal and Rajagopal 2011). At this stage, companies need to make heavy investment to develop brand awareness and value among customers. The overall performance may seem to be low, but reveals tendency of growth. Over a period, the new products should be driven by high perceived use values of customers to uplift the product at par with competing products. It is not easy for the firms to reach early breakeven points in business during the growth stage of product life cycle of relatively new products in the competitive markets. At this stage, companies need to invest on customer retention strategies, as competing products in the markets emerge as substitutes. Markets of high-technology products and services such as telecommunications and customer electronic appliances are highly influenced by fast technological changes and rapid generational substitutions. Since the conventional product development approaches based on market diffusion models do not usually incorporate this important aspect into their formulations, the accuracy of the provided forecasts is consequently affected (Michalakelis et al. 2010). The innovation diffusion, in the context of generation substitution, occurs due to the saturation of products in the market. Innovating a new product through collective intelligence and customer engagement is far broader project in scope than a simple process innovation within the acceptable technological framework. Successful companies ensure success by the following strategic touch points to make the new product a success in the competitive marketplace (Sawhney et al. 2006):

- Deliverables (customer solution, product attributes, complementarity, newness, affordability and adaptability)
- Venues (marketing platforms including brick-and-mortar and virtual platforms including corporate social media accounts)
- Products vs solutions (innovative solutions to the customer problems are more appealing in market as compared to unfamiliar innovations and new products)
- Customer segments (marketing innovative products in the ambidextrous market segments-premier and mass customer segments including niche markets)
- Experience sharing (sharing customer experiences through user-generated customer contents on social media channels to enhance customer outreach)
- Value chain management (customer value chain and supplier value chain management)
- Processes improvement (co-creation and simplification of production, operations, marketing, and customer relation management processes)
- Organizational behavior (work culture, commitment, employee and stakeholder engagement, decision making, performance management, and value enhancement)
- Streamlining supply-chain activities by redesigning logistics and inventory operations with a view to lower the transactional costs and increase profitability
- Making new products omnipresent in the brick-and-mortar and virtual marketplaces by streamlining supplies and services of the products
- Building product related e-space to give scope for customer interactions to encourage experience sharing
- Developing branding strategies for new products as flagship, shadow, or independent brand

Firms can benefit from opening up to the new idea development process to make competitive and effective decisions by integrating the principles of continuous innovation with the *stage gate* process. This process examines the potential opportunities of employing the principles of both inbound and outbound continuous innovation of a firm in both upstream and downstream marketplaces. The stage gate model can exploit the advantages of openness, spot rationale, and sustainable effect of decisions that are required in the marketplace. This model would allow explicit consideration of import and export of know-how and technology through gate evaluations and also enable firms to continuously assess their core capabilities and business model. A stage gate model is a conceptual and operational roadmap for moving a new-product project from idea to launch. This model divides the effort into distinct stages separated by management decision gates. Cross-functional teams must successfully complete a prescribed set of related cross-functional tasks in each stage prior to obtaining management approval to proceed to the next stage of product development. Stage gate processes have a great deal of appeal to management, because, basically, they restrict investment in the next stage until management is comfortable with the outcome of the current stage. The gate can be effective in controlling product quality and development expense. Stages-and-gates in the model function as sequential phases and may run into some overlapping activities, especially when they cross the decision points. The stage grate processes may not lead toward completing tasks in earlier phases to keep them off the critical path but they foster a mindset in which the work proceeds sequentially step by step. A newer alternative to stage gate process is the bounding box approach, which is essentially a management by exceptions technique, in which certain critical parameters of the project such as profit margin, project budget, product performance level, and launch date are negotiated as the bounding box. Firms need to conduct regular checks so that the process managers remain within bounds.

Summary

Companies engineer *design-to-market* strategies by mapping behavioral journeys of customers to gain competitive advantage for their products and services against other players. Successful companies have a precise organizational structure, with a manager accountable and strategist to map customer journey and earmark prominent touchpoints to consider in building competitive marketing strategy. Design-to-market has emerged as a contemporary business philosophy and a stimulated form to develop strategies compatible to target market. The hexagonal model of design-to-market philosophy illustrates the six core strategy areas comprising decision making, organizational control, functional factors, market attributes and competition, social interface of business, and co-creation. Most firms with successful implementation of design-to-market policies tend to map market attributes and the analyze competition ecosystem to deploy effective marketing strategies. The marketing-mix concept has been tested long by the companies and eventually it has become base of marketing theory. The hybrid marketing mix is combination of co-created marketing strategies and management of innovation and technology as strategy drivers. To improve the business performance and growth of the company within the vagaries of the competition, the elements of the marketing mix contribute effectively to the strengths and protect from competitive threats. Companies draw a strategy map based on selected marketing-mix elements, in the context of specific market scenarios to manage products and services in competitive markets. Such strategy map would get a picture of the competitive landscape of marketplace, which would educate managers to pick up a right marketing strategy with the combination of elements of marketing mix.

As customer preferences are changing rapidly, companies are developing design thinking in the strategies consider the competitive leverage over the time. Companies tend to reach customers and offer them competitive benefits through co-created organization practices and design. Shifts in the market processes in the society are induced by fundamental beliefs and shared assumptions and resemble elements of social culture defining norms of markets, expected behavior, and thought. Most firms know their customers sketchily and the marketing strategies are based on their innate assumption, competitive response, and rapid guesswork than scientific analysis of customer insights and strategic requirements. The rapid and abrupt shifts in consumer behavior has thrown major challenge to the customer-centric companies to achieve market competitiveness and consistent lead. The elements of marketing mix have evolved over the years in reference to the changing business environment, shifts in industry focus, and government regulations. Customer-centric businesses derive in-depth insights into what, how, and with whom customers want to interact during the co-creation process. Advances in digital technologies have augmented the scope of outsourcing business activities beyond geographic boundaries through several independent contributors. The collective insights develop co-created business models to drive an impact in emerging market through popular attributes of products, pricing, promotions, packaging, and managing customer psychodynamics based on collectively generated contents. Innovation of new products is a complex process that needs to be carried out meticulously in the firms integrating the business and customer use values in the marketplace.

Front-end activities comprising concept development, concept–design alignment, and concept commercialization allow customer-centric firms to validate strategies accordingly. Creativity is associated with the part of the innovation process that is labeled as idea generation. In planning for the product markets, it is essential to clearly understand the combinations of the expected margins and turnover in volume of the product. Customer satisfaction is perceived to be a key driver of the long-term relationship between the retailer and the customers, especially when customers are well acquainted with the products and markets, and when industries are highly competitive. Firms can benefit from opening up the new idea development process to make competitive and effective decisions by integrating the principles of continuous innovation with the *stage gate* process.

References

Aaker, D.A., and E. Joachimsthaler. 1999. "Lure of Global Branding." *Harvard Business Review* 77, no. 6, pp. 137–144.

Barczak, G., and K.B. Kahn. 2012. "Identifying New Product Development Best Practice." *Business Horizons* 55, no. 3, pp. 293–305.

Bhatt, G. 2000. "Organising Knowledge in the Knowledge Development Cycle." *Journal of Knowledge Management* 4, no. 1, pp. 15–26.

Bhattacharya, A.K., and D.C. Michael. 2008. "How Local Companies Keep Multinationals at Bay." *Harvard Business Review* 86, no. 3, pp. 84–95.

Bonabeau, E. 2009. "Decisions 2.0: The Power of Collective Intelligence." *MIT Sloan Management Review* 50, no. 2, pp. 45–52.

Bower, J.L., and T.M. Hout. 1988. "Fast-Cycle Capability for Competitive Power." *Harvard Business Review* 66, no. 6, pp. 110–118.

Bridgens, B., K. Hobson, D. Lilley, J. Lee, J.L. Scott, and G.T. Wilson. 2017. "Closing the Loop on E-Waste: A Multidisciplinary Perspective." *Journal of Industrial Ecology* 39, no. 1, pp. 1–13.

Brown, T. 2008. "Design Thinking." *Harvard Business Review* 86, no. 6, pp. 84–92.

D'Aveni, R.A. 2007. "Mapping Your Competitive Position." *Harvard Business Review* 85, no. 11, pp. 110–120.

Dawar, N., and C. Bagga. 2015. "A Better Way to Map Brand Strategy." *Harvard Business Review* 93, no. 6, pp. 90–97.

Edelman, D.C., and M. Singer. 2015. "Competing on Customer Journeys." *Harvard Business Review* 93, no. 11, pp. 88–100.

Floren, H., and J. Frishammar. 2012. "From Preliminary Ideas to Corroborated Product Definitions: Managing the Front End of New Product Development." *California Management Review* 54, no. 4, pp. 20–43.

Fuller, J. 2010. "Refining Virtual Co-Creation from a Customer Perspective." *California Management Review* 52, no. 2, pp. 98–122.

Gouillart, F., and D. Billings. 2013. "Community-Powered Problem Solving." *Harvard Business Review* 91, no. 4, pp. 70–77.

Gourville, J.T. 2006. "Eager Sellers and Stony Buyers: Understanding the Psychology of New-Product Adoption." *Harvard Business Review* 84, no. 6, pp. 98–106.

Handfield, R.B., G.L. Ragatz, K. Peterson, and R.M. Monczka. 1999. "Involving Suppliers in New Product Development." *California Management Review* 42, no. 1, pp. 59–82.

Hedaa, L., and T. Ritter. 2005. "Business Relationships on Different Waves: Paradigm Shift and Marketing Orientation Revisited." *Industrial Marketing Management* 34, no. 7, pp. 714–721.

Kumar, N. 2006. "Strategies to Fight Low-Cost Rivals." *Harvard Business Review* 84, no. 12, pp. 104–112.

Lamming, R.C., T.E. Johnsen, C.M. Harland, and J. Zheng. 2000. "Managing in Supply Networks: Cascade and Intervention." *9th International Annual IPSERA Conference,* University of Western Ontario, Canada, May 24–27.

Magids, S., A. Zorfas, and D. Leemon. 2015. "The New Science of Customer Emotions." *Harvard Business Review* 93, no. 11, pp. 66–76.

Michalakelis, C., D. Varoutas, and T. Sphicopoulos. 2010. "Innovation Diffusion with Generation Substitution Effects." *Technological Forecasting and Social Change* 77, no. 4, pp. 541–557.

Modaresnezhad, M., L. Iyer, P. Palvia, and V. Taras. 2020. "Information Technology (IT) Enabled Crowdsourcing: A Conceptual Framework." *Information Processing & Management* 57, no. 2, pp. 1–14.

Rajagopal, and A. Rajagopal. 2011. *Product Strategy and Six Sigma: Challenges, Convergence and Competence.* Hauppauge, New York, NY: Nova Science Publishers Inc.

Rajagopal. 2012. "Brand Manifestation and Retrieval Effects as Drivers of Buying Behavior in Mexico." *Journal of Database Marketing and Customer Strategy Management* 19,no. 3, pp. 179–196.

Rajagopal. 2015. *Butterfly Effect in Competitive Markets: Driving Small Change for Larger Differences.* Basingstoke, UK: Palgrave Macmillan.

Rajagopal. 2019. *Contemporary Marketing Strategy: Analyzing Consumer behavior to Drive Managerial Decision Making.* New York, NY: Palgrave Macmillan.

Rajagopal. 2020. *Market Entropy: How to Manage Chaos and Uncertainty for Improving Organizational Performance.* New York, NY: Business Expert Press.

Shapiro, B.P. 1985. "Rejuvenating the Marketing Mix." *Harvard Business Review* 63, no. 5, pp. 28–34.

Slater, S.F., E.M. Olson, and G.T.M. Hult. 2010. "Worried about Strategy Implementation? Don't overlook Marketing's Role." *Business Horizons* 53, no. 5, pp. 469–479.

Sawhney, M., R.C. Wolcott, and I. Arroniz. 2006. "12 Different Ways for Companies to Innovate." *MIT Sloan Management Review* 47, no. 3, pp. 75–81.

Robson, K., and S. Beninger. 2016. *Does Mattel's Iconic Barbie Doll Need a Makeover?* Boston: Harvard Business Publishing.

Tsai, S.P. 2005. "Integrated Marketing as Management of Holistic Customer Experience." *Business Horizons* 48, no. 5, pp. 431–441.

Tsai, C. 2019. "The Needs-Adaptive Customer: Understanding How and Why People Shop." *Rotman Management Magazine*, pp. 1–6.

Tauscher, K. 2017. "Leveraging Collective Intelligence: How to Design and Manage Crowd-Based Business Models." *Business Horizons* 60, no. 2, pp. 237–245.

CHAPTER 3

Design-to-Society

Overview

The theory of social engagement and social presence endorses the design-to-society philosophy in business modeling. This chapter discusses the conceptual and functional perspectives of social marketing and focuses on design-to-society approach by describing the interactive path, business and society convergence, policy implications, and society-driven growth. The effects of social networks and collective communication on business modeling in the context of user-generated contents are addressed in this chapter. In addition, a discussion on the social impact of media communication on business and toward developing core competencies supplements the design-to-society concept. This chapter also illustrates the co-creation and coevolution within the ecosystem of social business modeling through real business examples, graphics, and conceptual frameworks.

The growth in the information technologies and popularity of the social media channels have helped most customer-centric companies promote their products and create social value. Companies have gone the extra mile to derive collective intelligence, document customer experience, and draw value map on the basis of user-generated contents. Their presence on the social media has brought together friends and followers on social platforms such as Facebook, and few have succeeded in performing social marketing on media channels making profits. However, these companies selectively port their digital strategies into social ecosystem by broadcasting their commercial messages and general value out of the community feedback. The focus of design-to-society business modeling is to evolve business through the people by developing social strategies in tune with the customers, and stakeholders' expectations, and connect them with the company to coevolve business. For example, many companies such as Amazon, American Express, Nestlé, and Unilever exhibits the success of social strategies that have complemented to profits by creating social value. Hindustan Unilever Ltd has effectively implemented the Shakti program in India to empower rural women to generate social values and demonstrate performance with purpose. Such social connection helps the company in customer acquisition, marketing, and content creation (Piskorski 2011).

Social engagement is a socially responsive approach in managing tasks and socioeconomic practices with expected outcomes. Social engagement aligns with individual, community, civic, and institutional benefits including leveraging the benefits from business and economy. While social scholarship focuses on the individual and community attributes as a state of engagement, the social perspective of engagement endorses collective impact on co-created businesses through a socially determined process. The design-to-society philosophy is, therefore, aligned with the social engagement theory and social presence maxim, which refers to the degree of presence perceived by the community participants in generating and disseminating communication. Social presence theory argues that social media (physical and digital interactions) should align with psychological perception of involvement (presence) and transmit visual and verbal cues. Social presence broadly includes the activities of sharing ideas and experiences, communicating social postures, social brand expressions, social needs, upholding customer voice, and monitoring checks and balances on business to society value transfers (Calefato and Lanubile 2010).

Social Marketing

Social marketing platforms have increasingly involved customers not only in communication, but also in designing the social websites of companies. The active roles of stakeholders in community interactions and experience sharing have helped companies in co-creating products and services, and user-generated marketing content to enhance the market competitiveness of their products and services. Many social media customer groups have become strategic partners to the companies in socializing the brands and synchronizing the social, cultural, and ethnic values of customers with the market trends. For example, Bimbo bread company in Mexico has been using social media platforms to promote its brands since long, and in the recent past, it has created a social media platform for the football fans using the celebrity players to promote its sandwich bread brands. Such strategy, integrating the social interests and culture, is synchronized with the design-to-society business model of the company. Similarly, social media platforms have become the cornerstone of the marketing strategies of most fashion companies. Smart businesses recognize just how prevalent social media is in the lives of their customer base. The impact of social media on fashion industry is evident from its enhanced outreach to customers and market competitiveness. Fashion companies and their brands have been successful in leveraging the voice of customers on digital social networks and the fashion designs to make direct appeal to the customers in the market. Customer-centric companies develop social marketing programs and campaigns to reach customers to create awareness on brands, promote brands at the competitive edge, and enhance their brand experience on real time. However, some companies with less expertise in the digital networks like YouTube, Facebook, Instagram, and Twitter are too often treated as stand-alone elements rather than part of an integrated business system (Hanna et al. 2008).

Social media applications including collaborative projects, micro-blogs, blogs, content communities, social networking sites, and virtual worlds have become part of the standard communication repertoire for many companies. The creation of powerful mobile devices has elevated the growth opportunities for numerous social media applications to go mobile. With the advancement of information technology services and growing interest of customers on managing communication with the electronic devices, the socialization of brands, emotions, and decision making among customers are getting synchronized, culminating in the business models today. Consequently, the expectations on the performance of brands are rising high among customers. Hence, firms are exploring the social purpose of the brands beyond mere functional benefits and the companies are taking apparent social stances to create social value for their business. Such socialization of brands, corporate involvement in social development through the corporate social responsibility, and inculcating the business philosophy of performance with purpose are significantly contributing to the design-to-society perspectives of business modeling. Broadly, the design-to-society attributes are integrated with the design-to-market business philosophy.

The design-to-society approach is founded on the value-based business thinking, which explains the concepts of "competing with social purpose" and "performance with purpose" underlying in the welfare marketing business school of thought. The combination of design-to-society and design-to-market business philosophies connect social aspirations including the customer values to persuade market-growth needs of the companies. An effective social strategy tagged with the brand value fortifies the business goals and means. Nonetheless, it mitigates the risk of passive social associations and radical conceptualization of means to achieve performance and poses threats to stakeholder acceptance of society-linked business models. The stakeholder value can be created for all stakeholders, customers, the company, and the community at large through strategic pursuit of brand marketing and corporate goals (Rodriguez-Vila and Bharadwaj 2017).

A social media activist may have a mix of experience with product design, marketing, software applications, and the extended reach of the communication. Companies should analyze customer experience centered on social interactions to develop community-linked marketing approaches. Such customer connectivity helps the managers stay on social media platforms like Facebook page and work with the social media account management, and social advertising and social media campaign management that are the typical customer-centric marketing tasks for a company. As the social networks are growing fast and gaining psychodynamics, there emerges the need for a new executive-level position in firms as the social marketing strategist, who can fully embrace the focus on social marketing. Social consciousness and business are growing simultaneously among the customers and stakeholders as a result of the ease of use of technology and transformation of communication systems form conventional wisdom to digital networks. Corporate social responsibility has become the tool to generate social consciousness and value streams to support social marketing perspectives of business. Public policies and the media have become proficient to stimulate the companies to take initiatives in developing social markets and inculcating the social consequences in the future business modeling to grow their business with the social outlooks. Consequently, the social face of business has emerged as an inescapable priority form the customer-centric companies to gain competitive leverage. Some successful business-to-customer companies like Amazon discovered Whole Foods as a social business place to generate social values and drive the business growth faster. Similarly, Toyota, and Volvo have found design-to-society approaches in business more as source of innovation and competitive advantage than a path of smooth transition of technology-oriented business in the society. Companies, while developing social imperatives in business, need to identify the social consequences of their actions and discover opportunities to benefit society and themselves by strengthening the competitive benefits. The design-to-society business modeling has, therefore, emerged as a collective thinking mindset for strategic growth of business through the social value stream (Porter and Kramer 2006).

Companies should develop social media strategies on the basis of *hub and spoke model*, where a hub is located around social media. The *hub* may be led by the corporate social strategist to monitor the core communication movements within the networks and draw a framework of marketing strategy integrating customer attributes and corporate policy. The hub marketing framework needs to be further converged with the functionaries accountable in various departments of the company that denotes *spokes* in the model. New applications for the mobile social networking platforms are constantly appearing in the market, which have tempted many companies to tap the social network activities also from the mobile devices. A mobile device is any tool that allows access to a ubiquitous network beyond one specific access gate. The most common example of mobile device is mobile phone, but a netbook also counts if it can access different types of wireless networks such as WLAN, and 3G (Kaplan 2012). Design-to-society is a community approach in developing market ecosystem on the social foundation. Most companies invest in creating social value by co-creating corporate social responsibility and developing public–private partnership by working on a social cause. Though the corporate investment in design-to-society has a long-run payback, it could play tactical in managing market competition through the social value inputs of the business. Costs and benefits of the social investment of business from the perspective of targeted growth in the marketplace often poses many challenges. Design-to-society approach to targeted community provides a significant benefit to the customers and stakeholders over the conventional for-profit marketing methods. However, in some cases, such as in sustainability projects, the social investment involves high cost in terms of either money or intangible measure (difficulty, for instance, in quitting smoking); it becomes harder for the company to connect the payback to the existing revenue streams. Social marketers face their greatest challenge in converging the intangible social benefits with business growth and performance with purpose (Rangan et al. 1996).

Social media, enveloping several customer networks across the regions in the world, has rapidly gained share and attention among mass customers and companies, often at the cost of traditional media. Hence, most companies have started to redefine key aspects of their marketing mix considering the activities of the informal networks of customers. With advertising and online word-of-mouth competing for the shrinking marketing budgets, many companies consider having an active presence in social media as a viable alternative to traditional advertising. A comparison of advertising and word-of-mouth shows that social media follows rules that are very different from traditional advertising. Social media can start conversations or build brand recognition, but the results are much more difficult to predict or measure (Armelini and Villanueva 2011).

Information technologies, social innovations, and social marketing are growing as a triadic force converging both business models and social values. The triadic effect is revolutionizing products, services, and consumer behavior in all industrial segments. The mechanical and electrical products such as conventional audio-visual equipment have become complex systems combining hardware, sensors, electronics, and software that connect through the internet in numerous ways. These smart, connected products have penetrated the society by offering exponentially expanding opportunities for new businesses that transcend traditional product boundaries. Social technologies are forcing marketers to form new kinds of relationships with customers, but traditional brand management models are different for these new kinds of interactions between companies and customers. Brand marketers need to update their models to include new-media mentors, who are digitally knowledgeable executives and who intend to move fast, understand how to integrate social media into corporate communications, and can organize cross-functional teams (Spenner 2010). Most companies are rethinking on their business models to induct smart technologies in social ecosystem. Accordingly, the products and markets are conceived to match design-to-market and design-to-society perspectives, and source their products to manufacturing, operating, and service providing agencies. Companies build and secure the necessary business infrastructure through co-creation and coevolution. Smart, connected products offer a broad set of new strategic choices in the society to generate value with new partnerships to secure competitive advantage and restructure market boundaries with enhanced capabilities (Porter and Heppelmann 2014).

During the traditional marketing (nondigital) practices, companies used to monitor and respond to community activities through customer relations employees giving a personal touch. Such interpersonal practices helped companies meticulously implement customer outreach strategy and improve social skills and adaptive tactics. However, digitized social media platforms have enhanced the power of communities by promoting relations over time and space (geodemographic) and facilitated rapid customer engagement. The experience sharing of customers and stakeholder, and illustrating their creativity on the digital platforms not only improve the customer engagement in business, but also grow collective information and knowledge. The social media participation has attracted customer participation voluntarily and in an unconditional charter, which influences business strategies significantly. On the social media, health websites are managed by both public institutions (government help departments) and private organizations, where people share details about their illness and the treatments they've pursued, their need for revised diagnosis, and treatment. Members and medical experts exchange their ideas and develop initial relations as gateways for hospitalization or continuing with the in-person treatments. Tata Health has launched social health website and Instadoc application for PC and mobile devices. The social health websites visualize complex health histories of patients and allow comparisons and feedback among peers to develop a mindset on the health problems. Customer-centric companies encourage social teams to explore co-created business opportunities and develop brand value (Kane et al. 2009).

The pharmaceutical industry provides a good example of interventions of social networks in marketing. It has been observed that social networks play a key role in doctors' prescribing choices. Doctors tend to be slow to recommend a drug despite it has been proven effective and patients, and pharmacists often wait until the doctors they trust start doing so. Studies have shown that physicians were much more likely to prescribe the diabetes medication Januvia if they had Januvia adopters in their networks. Social connections can also work the other way, turning physicians away from certain drugs. Sales of Pfizer's cholesterol drug Lipitor declined quickly when a generic medication the US market. Consequently, interconnected doctors switched their prescriptions accordingly to the low-price brand *Vitales* of the company in the Mexican market. The drug industry is an apparent place for the activists of social networks to comments on drugs, doctors, and hospitals (Miller and Christakis 2011). Social network analysis is valuable in facilitating collaboration among various strategic groups in the company such as leadership networks, strategic business units, new product development teams, communities of practice, joint ventures, and mergers. By making informal networks visible, social network analysis helps managers systematically assess and support strategically important collaboration (Cross et al. 2002).

The key to effective social marketing is conversing with and listening to the people the company is trying to reach. Social marketing is a customer-driven process, and all aspects of marketing program must be developed considering the needs of the target audience as the central focus. In order to learn what customers want, it is necessary to make them express. Good marketers know that there is no such thing as selling to the general public. Customers respond differently to particular approaches and to be most effective, audiences may be segmented into homogeneous groups and create messages specifically for each segment. The communications should be rendered precisely to the target groups analyzing information about their needs and perceptions about the products and services. A company may also segment customers on the basis of their knowledge about the products and services. For example, a new taste of food may be targeted to the segment who has never tasted the specific food, instead of to those who have. However, people still vary greatly within these segments; but the more specific it can get, the greater will be the potential impact.

In social marketing, products are often hard to promote because of their high price. Products that need to develop customers' attitude require long-term commitments. The product positioning determines how the target audience thinks about the product as compared to the substitutes. The company may develop promotion strategies and reinforce the attributes of the products that add to the perceived value of the customers. In the commercial sector, successful companies watch every move their competitors make. They know their selling environment intimately and are ready to react as soon as conditions change. Social marketers also need to be aware of the competing messages pulling on their target audiences. Just as Coke creates its marketing strategies based on what Pepsi is doing, companies can take advantage of their competitors' tactics to promote their own products. Many successful campaigns against tobacco and alcohol have satirized the well-known cigarette and beer slogans, creating ads that grab attention because of their new twist on familiar images. Other environmental factors may also affect people's reactions to the promotion campaigns and sales program.

People do not go out of their way to find corporate messages or promotion bulletins. The messages need to be put in places that can be accessed by target audience. While conversing with the potential customers on social network platforms, they should be tinkled to reveal where they get their news, what radio stations they listen to online, and where they go in their free time. In case the target audience tends to read the local newspaper, it would be the right way to place the communication there and work with that business journalists to get coverage in both print and social media. Social marketing involves much more than television advertising campaigns. The most effective programs use a combination of mass media, community, and small group and individual activities. When a simple, clear message is repeated in many places and formats throughout the community, it is more likely to be seen and remembered. A social marketing program might contain Internet blogging platforms and radio spots, community event, a poster contest, giveaways of products or coupons, and a toll-free hotline for individual counseling on the products and services of the company. It is important for the companies to know that customers do not buy products in true sense, they buy solutions. Hence, the company should learn the problems lying with the customers through the social networks before presenting the products.

Design-to-Society Approach

Social values are founded in the customer cognition process, which stimulate customers on knowing about the brands, doing with the prescribed brand purpose, and attaining perceived value and satisfaction being a conscious customer. The factors of knowing, doing, and being form the core of design-to-society approach. Understanding the attributes, personality, corporate image, and prescribed values of brands, customers tend to increasingly evaluate the social and consumption purpose of the brands to have a social purpose beyond mere functional benefits. As a result, companies are taking social stands to build business models on social welfare and development philosophies. For example. Lego, the Danish brand, has developed a steady and strong presence in the market by developing a coherent storyline on sustainability, education, and societal contributions to generate value. The company is in the process of replacing the chemical plastic materials with bio-plastics. The bio-plastic is developed from wheat straw, bamboo fiber, rice husks, sugarcane, corn starch, and other plant resources. The new stream of bio-plastics is being explored with polylactic acids (PLAs), which naturally occur in plants, or polyhydroxy alkenoates (PHAs) engineered from microorganisms. Such transformation in manufacturing the building blocks of Lego has instilled a social posture in the company, which has helped in regaining the brand value through convergence of design-to-society and design-to-market philosophies in business modeling. Such design-to society programs benefit both society and the brand strategically to establish brand competitiveness and social push to the brand. However, investing in design-to-society programs to inculcate social values in brand without appropriate design-to-market approaches might reduce the expected growth, profits, and business expansion of companies. The design-to-society approaches provide the companies the scope for competing in market with a social purpose by exhibiting the most ambitious social aspirations brands with the desired spatial and temporal growth touchpoints (Rodriguez-Vila and Bharadwaj 2017).

In view of the growing competition in the different layers of marketplaces from urban markets to the bottom-of-the-pyramid segments, most companies slowly understand the significance of the role of social media in developing marketing strategies. Most companies have developed a parallel communication channel around the social media along with their business propositions. Hence, the emerging firms feel that there should be a social marketing strategist who needs to play the role in stimulating discussion in the media, filtering communications, picking new ideas, and analyzing opportunities for co-creation of strategies with the customers. The role of social media strategist should be to develop customer-centric approaches for the company and integrate social experiences into products and services. Co-creation is a continuous process of collaborative efforts between society, customers, stakeholders, and the company. Optimal collaborations focus on new product development through frugal or incremental innovations, and on improving business processes and market performance. The societal involvement begins in a small scale (home base) with a small group of social participants and key organization(s). Upon drafting the project charter and business model, products and services are marketed by embedding social values and benefits with shared interest, which encourages market competitiveness. The convergence of design-to-society and design-to-market enables quick wins, and builds customers' trust on brands. To manage such lead in the business, co-creation and customer engagement are able to co-create new dimensions within the fragile and complex market ecosystem (Nidumolu et al. 2014). The social media strategists figure out the existing relationships of customers with companies and determine the ways to bring out those relationships into the experiences of every product and service of the company. The social strategist ensures to build new social experiences and embracing customer experiences with the company and makes the customers stay on the network platforms with their friends and family. The attributes of design-to-market approach and their interactive path is illustrated in Figure 3.1.

Integration of social and business ecosystems with focus on business and society in the respective domains encourages smooth conversation of design-to-society and design-to-market attributes as illustrated in Figure 3.1. The design-to-society attributes today are transforming from conventional wisdom to digital tools to socialize brands and deliver social values. The digital interactions among customers help companies socialize brands

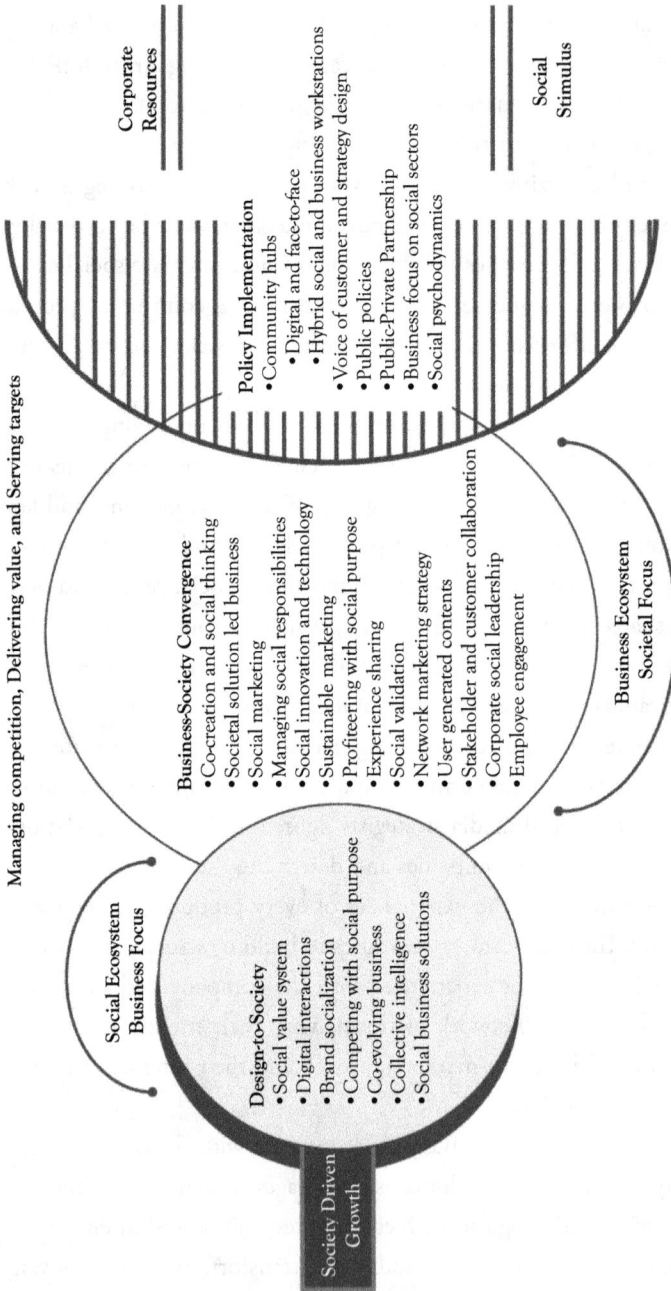

Figure 3.1 Interactive path of design-to-market attributes

Source: Author.

and create brand value for competitive leverage. Socialization of marketing strategies, innovations, and brands drives collective impact among customers, which strengthens the competitive positions of companies in the marketplace. The collective impact has enabled many successful collaborations in the social health, education, small enterprises, energy, and agricultural sector by guiding businesses and blending the ecosystems to deliver solutions and create value. In the process, companies explored economic opportunities to ride over the competitive hurdles. The collective impact is generated with a common agenda between the society and the companies to align design-to-market approaches within the social ecosystems, which helps in aligning business operations and commitments. Creating and delivering values from business to society needs a shared measurement system that reinforces activities between the stakeholders, customers, and the company. In addition, user-generated contents derived from the social platform require appropriate filters to highlight consistent and value-based communication, which builds trust and ensures establishing the mutual goals. Nonetheless, linking society with business operations needs a dedicated support of the employees, corporate management, stakeholders, customers, suppliers and other players in business operations. Involving society with business is a synchronized process of communication transfers, resource sharing, creating public will, integrating social and business infrastructure, and aligning corporate social objectives with the public policies (Kramer and Pfitzer 2016). Consequently, companies develop competitive strategies aligning social purposes and coevolve business to deliver the social business solutions. In this process, companies widely benefit from the social knowledge pool and collective intelligence.

The business and society convergence are supported by the transformational (change in social thinking) and transactional (value-based philosophy) thinking by cocreating solutions to the societal problems related to business sector. Social marketing strategies are the effective tools to align business goals with social development and value generation perspectives. Social innovations, sustainable development, green marketing, and implementing corporate social responsibility programs stimulate enhancement of performance with social purpose. This linear path bridging the gap between society and business validates the design-to-society

and design-to-market philosophies. Social validation of marketing programs by sharing customer experiences on the digital platforms and generating user-driven contents develop scope of co-creation of products and
services effectively within the society and market. Sustainable customer
products companies like IKEA, GE Energy, and Unilever focus on inducing corporate social leadership in managing the corporate social responsibility. However, while implementing society-linked business models,
companies tend to develop community hubs for customer and stakeholder interactions on face-to-face, digital, or hybrid communication
models. The interactions of customer on these platforms help companies
document the voice of customers to support strategy designs. In addition,
public policies, public–private partnerships, and social psychodynamics
leverage companies in designing programs to evolve in vulnerable social
sectors (health, education, housing, agriculture, and nonfarm economic
production, with meticulous business strategies.

A good social strategy for a company requires an analysis of all internal marketing and sales assets. In this way, the company can gather up all
customer/client-facing online content, including policy papers, published
reports, presentations, messaging, online videos, and mobile applications.
In order to get close involvement with the social media, a company needs
to list all relevant contents appearing on blogs, any on-site communities,
Facebook, and Twitter, to inculcate an active discussion. To be an effective
and hassle-free involvement with the social networks, a company should
assess what has been communicated (content types, length, and messaging
per target), and how, and how often, it has been communicated with the
network users. In order to work with social media platforms, business-driv-
ing keywords need to be identified and set onto the search engines by the
company. A periodical review of how the lead has been taken should also
be done to restore the visibility through social networks and search engine
optimization (SEO) program results. The SEO program results are related
to the social marketing activity and its effectiveness in reference to the company as an anchor. Social media marketing is the ultimate communications
tool for reaching and engaging a target audience in the following ways:

- Excellent customer service
- Updates on brand, products, and services

- Product and service promotions
- Education of the customer around the corporate value
- Letting the brand go online with the social networks
- Looking for crowdsourcing to pick up potential social networks as brand ambassadors
- Acting as a think-tank by taking the lead in online customer education

There are many reasons social media can be a productive marketing channel or platform. Rather than employing it as a tactic, the purpose should dictate the strategy and the tactics used for reaching desired goals. A few common outcomes for social media marketing efforts are detailed as follows (Rajagopal 2013):

- *Gain insight into a community of interest*
  A company can run many customer surveys online, but some of the most interesting and progressive market research can be found within the social communities where customers interact, share information, and make recommendations. Monitoring and analyzing various social media streams and engaging into the active dialogues with customer are more challenging for firms. To stay engaged in the effective social participation and portray the corporate image of the company to generate awareness about the brands, companies believe in developing design-to-society strategies.
- *Build brand visibility and authority*
  In the global marketplace, markets are open, and customers interact without boundaries about a company's products, brands and services across the network platforms. Thus, companies should intervene in the social media and participate in the conversations about its products, brands, and services, and streamline the discussions.
- *Influence and promotion of products or services*
  It would be a good idea for the companies to provide adequate information to educate customers about products and services in the formats and media types they prefer.

The relationship of a company with social networks can go a long way toward building business sensitivity that results into strengthening the status of the company against its competitors.

- *Analyze the network traffic*

  Creating discussion link to a blog and promoting it to social media news, and allowing auto bookmarking sites can attract bloggers from various social networks to participate in the activities of the company. However, high levels of promotion in the same site or communicating frequently with the unfamiliar user accounts could make the association of social networks ineffective and turn the communications as social media spam. Creating value for the community is not the only rule, creating value and behaving according to the formal and informal rules is what sustains social media link building.

- *Drive traffic for revenue models*

  Becoming a user of homogeneous social communities involves consistently contributing quality content and rewarding those who respond positively on the posting, and growing large base followers through attractive initiatives. Such base of concurring connections can serve as an effective distribution channel for unique and interesting contents, which drives traffic to ad-supported blogs that host the content. Companies that would like to use the social media actively may also consider turning on *link bait strategy* (advertisements that have perennial links). The link bait not only attracts links but also attracts traffic. However, many sites supported by advertisements report that traffic from social media sites is disreputable for not clicking on links. The link bait strategy includes creating visuals with website links, focusing on core functions of the company, listing social media links (forums, communities, and blogs) for providing quick customer solutions, website layout optimization, and capitalizing on voice of customers (reviews and feedback).

Effective social networking on digital and face-to-face interactions enables companies to design network marketing. Engaging customers in marketing process drives psychodynamics and enhances the scope of peer-review-led brand building. Direct marketing and retailing companies largely view sales networks in terms of direct contacts and often depend upon the social networks. However, the companies intensively involved with customers like financial services may not necessarily have an effective network because networks often pay off their value through indirect contacts. Moreover, a thumb rule in customer-centric companies is to adopt relevant social networks and let them grow with the support of the company so that it can embark on such platforms to gain competitive advantage in the marketplace. Hence, density of the connections in a network is important. However, thin networks are also better for generating unique information. By increasing investment in social media by network marketing, companies like Mary Kay Cosmetics engage customers also as sellers both in the face-to-face and digital forums. With the growing interest of mobile marketing among customers, the digital networks like Facebook have become widely used forums, and exhibit real transactional emotions in the virtual marketplace. However, social networks have yet to emerge as a fully functional vehicle for building customer loyalty, and as a cognitive platform to create brand awareness. Marketing though Facebook helps in increasing loyalty by integrating personal beliefs and trust with public opinions to reinforce customer satisfaction, perceived value, and commitment toward a brand. Such experiment has been a success for the high-value fashion brands in apparel, cosmetics, and perfumes. Such personal–public blend in brand relations is growing strong for followers of the brand, which inculcates loyalty overtime among customers in the society (Gamboa and Goncalves 2014).

Managers can use direct marketing structure, comparative compensation, and competitive skill development strategies, to encourage, monitor, and evaluate enthusiastic customer-sellers to adopt a network-based view for effectively using the social network platforms. For instance, the sales force can be restructured to delink lead generation from other tasks because some people are very good at building diverse ties but not so good at maintaining other kinds of networks. Companies that take steps of this kind to help their marketing and sales teams build better networks and reap competitive advantages (Ustuner and Godes 2006). In view of the several successful efforts of the virtual-platform companies like Google and Amazon, the emerging business organizations should start considering the role of social product strategist into their organizations' social media strategy. Most companies seek product-focused managers who demonstrate strong experience in building social user experiences into the products they work with, and are able to manage the up-front social networks like Facebook and Twitter applications and experiences. The social media strategist should also have a proven understanding of the benefits of social design into company's products. The design-to-society philosophy lays foundation for design-to market and design-to-value thinking. However, companies face a major challenge in screening, classifying, and responding to the public opinions in the process of socializing the business. Many companies, which explore marketing and business opportunities through the digital community platforms, are often unable to exploit the information to a full extent. The social media impacts entrepreneurial, financial, operational, and corporate social performance. Interactions within social channels develop social capital, disseminate customer preferences, and help social marketing. Broadly, the social networking drives the companies in building appropriate society-driven business model. On social media, the number of "followers" and volume of "likes" positively influence shared values of the company and attract critical masses toward the shared and user-generated contents (Paniagua and Sapena 2014).

Social networks also help firms go sustainable by building loyalty and trust corporate policies. Successful sustainable enterprises in developing countries often involve informal networks that include businesses, nonprofit organizations, and local communities. These networks prompt the firms to go for investments in in the financial, social, human, and ecological capital areas. Successful sustainable networks require business enterprises to sponsor for ensuring the network's financial sustainability and serve as the anchor of the company. Multinational corporations sometimes support social networks to anchor with specific operational objectives (Wheeler et al. 2005). Google has done this well, it has tried to embrace social media. Many know Google for taking a developer-centric focus around the products it builds. It has encompassed this philosophy in the knowledge dissemination vision of the company to figure out the challenges around social product design within the organization. Accordingly, Google proceeded to create a new network Google+ to get the entire organization reveal the real relationships their users have. This integrated platform has also given a face-lift to the Google product line and its application. It has emerged as a product design strategy of the company.

Social Networks, Communications, and Business Modeling

Understanding social needs is an essential challenge for the companies to create social value by delivering right solutions. In order to dive deep into the social needs, communication is critical to explore the social cognition, and construct strategic or tactical solutions. Therefore, social participation through active engagement is the underlying requirement for most customer-centric companies. Marketing today is evolving inside the participatory conversations with customers and stakeholders. Precise, positive, promotional, and personality-building marketing communications with distinct and identifiable brand or corporate focus provide a streamlined path for the social conversation on business modeling. However, chaotic market-oriented communications with multitarget audiences spread across customers, competitors, observers, and employees affect the strategy implementation and decision systems across the market players within the industry (Muñiz and Schau 2011). Brand communities have grown along the corporate site for sharing experiences of variety-seeking customers in the context of value-based activities. The communally seeded and empowered customers are now a marketplace reality as they portray social needs, preferences, and values on the business canvas. The social networks help companies in business modeling in the following ways:

- Sharing positive or negative experience
- Illustrating the unconscious biasness of customer toward brands and corporate strategies
- Building user-generated contents
- Evolving the social and ethnic trends (food, fashion, and social products)
- Delivering ethnographic analysis of customer, society, and brand coexistence

- Developing social marketing campaigns
- Mapping systematic social cognition to support business modeling decisions
- Showcasing homegrown advertisements with verbal and nonverbal contents, and
- Facilitating virtual collaborations with managers of the firm on developing strategies or resoling social issues in business.

Design-to-society approaches offer a vigilant marketing system to gain competitive leverage in the market by integrating the social business process. Many marketers actively solicit user-generated content (UGC) on various food (diet, alcohol, and organic products) and fashion (apparel and accessories) products for occasional and short-term use in advertising campaign. Accordingly, the UGC are successfully integrated into broad objectives of firms to harmoniously co-produce the brand content, which is recommended for the innovation and service-dominant logic (Vargo and Lusch 2004).

Most efforts to promote corporate social network collaboration are chaotic and built on the implicit philosophy that the higher the connectivity, the better the performance of an organization. It is challenging for executives to learn how to promote connectivity only where it benefits an organization or individual, and how to decrease unnecessary connections. The customized response network excels at reducing the redundancy in communication and filters out the ambiguous problems involved in innovative thinking on business strategy specific conversations with the customers. Strategy consulting firms and new product development groups tend to work on this format. Managers need to develop a strategic view of the collaboration with social network participants within the policy of the company, which supports the types of social networks that best fit their goals (Cross et al. 2005).

Increased mobility in brick-and-mortar and virtual space in the marketplace has prompted higher peer interactions through the social networks. Consequently, new ideas in business and innovative concerns are increasingly shared in a niche market or social networks, which often open the corporate boundaries for creating customer value and pro-customer business modeling. Informal networks, though small in size, provide both strategic opportunity and potential threat, while they can increase creativity within a firm. Informal social networks like person-oriented or brand-led blogs are growing manifold. Companies or business associations need to recognize relevant informal social networks to collect quality information. Validation of information communication networks has emerged as major challenge as the communication embedded therein might damage the brand image or corporate reputation. Managing unrecognized social networks is sensitive for many firms as they help firms in the diffusion of creative knowledge to other firms through personnel and knowledge transfer on one hand, but are susceptible to information infidelity on the other. Firms that operate within small worlds, such as information technology-based services firms, fell in to such damage caused by the social networks. Most firms have learned long ago to manage innovation prompted by the unorganized social networks that were grown in isolation. However, all firms now need to learn how to manage innovation and improvement in the existing business in a small world environment of virtual social networks (e.g., Fleming and Marx 2006). With the increase in the market competition, most organizations have begun to embrace the idea that understanding the problem and formulation of the solution are woven around different kinds of conversations. Problem structuring is a critical aspect of the design process that can be comprehensively contributed by the social networks (Conklin and Christinsen 2009).

Before companies enter the workstations of new mobile devices, tablets, and personal computers stimulating the social networks, it is necessary to perform quality checks with the Internet search engines. Internet connections to drive social media strategy with the company. As a key performance engine for client/customer engagement, social media activity considers all organizational activities including marketing and sales. Thus, companies planning to be customer-centric and bringing the social networks in their business gamut should integrate their sales teams, marketing teams, social teams, creative teams, brand ambassadors, and communication anchors on a single platform to develop a social marketing strategy. The smartest way to move on this is to appoint one network coordinator in the company to lead the customer relation and be accountable for social media marketing goals and communicating any internal policies of the company.

Measuring the social impact of networks and their alliances by a social entrepreneurial organization is driven by its capabilities in the areas of staffing, communication, alliance building, and stimulating market forces. The relative importance of each of these capabilities in driving scaling depends on several situational contingencies, such as the escalated market demand, or change of product distribution policies (Bloom and Chatterji 2009). Social networks are also proved to be good resources for companies to administer the corporate social responsibility projects. Most companies involve social networks and social media in managing the social projects as communication interface. Such social platforms are very effective in socializing the corporate brands. Companies are increasingly considering corporate social responsibility as a key to the long-term success in the market and bridging the ties with the society by collaborating with nonprofit organizations and social networks in various ways to establish themselves as good corporate citizens. Social networks help the companies in driving social alliances with focus on long-term collaborations to achieve strategic objectives for both organizations. Although social alliances pose structural problems, they can be designed, structured, nurtured, and maintained in a manner that enables the companies and the society to contribute to solving the pressing social problems and driving companies' image in the society by ways of corporate social responsibility (Berger et al. 2004).

Firms, irrespective of their size, are leaning toward nurturing the strategic alliances using social networks to gain competitive advantage. The cooperative relationships are driven by the firms to excel their competencies, safeguard resources, share risks, be dynamic to get into new markets, and create attractive options for future investments. However, many alliances fail to meet the expectations because nurturing the working relationships and interpersonal connections that tie the partnering organizations with customer community are not considered by the companies seriously. Such company–customer personal relationships serve to shape and modify the evolving public–private partnership and help in building corporate social image. While developing social alliances by the companies, streamlining the discussions on social platforms is a significant task for the managers (Dyer et al. 2001). The flow of communication from the social networks on predetermined platforms, and the proactive, reactive, and interactive exchange of information can be strengthened by nurturing cooperative relationships in several ways. An effective corporate collaboration with social networks should be built in pyramidal hierarchy comprising top management to develop broad goals and monitor progress, middle managers to develop charter of collaborative activities with social networks, and, at the bottom, the organization operational personnel to get involved with the community while carrying out the routine tasks. Integrating social communities in the corporate strategy and operational activities would build the organization stronger (Hutt et al. 2000). The common competencies that can be judged in reference to the competitor are as follows:

- Quick movement of the products to the marketplace from community place
- Faster response to the market opportunities
- Providing convincing and unique solutions to the customer problems
- Hire, train, and retain best personnel
- Develop, nurture, and extend the best relationship with customers and alliance partners

There are four key tasks in the management of core competence: selecting core competence, building core competence, deploying core competence, and protecting core competence. Companies are likely to differ in terms of their abilities to select, build, deploy, and protect core competence. These differences are, in turn, likely to yield differences in corporate performance. Building core competence requires the accumulation and integration of knowledge within the firm. For example, a telecom company's core competence in managing billing systems, an insurance company's core competence in claims processing, and Sony's core competence in miniaturization, are built around technologies and operational skills. The core competencies of the companies are those that push down the competitors' products in all the business domains. These strategies are central to the customers, channels, and alliance advantage.

The social networks, composed of innumerous groups of customers worldwide that are attempting to address critical social and marketing needs, have long been regarded as incompatible for the companies in guiding their business. The profit-oriented customer-centric companies now have an opportunity to collaborate with social networks to create new markets for reaching the four billion people who are not yet a part of the world's formal economy. The power of such collaborations lies in the complementary strengths of the partners including the scale of manufacturing, financing, and retailing. Social entrepreneurs offer lower costs, strong social networks, and deep insights into potential customers and communities, and set up hybrid value chain. This framework may be defined as the hybrid value chain. For example, Elekta, a customer durables retail company in Mexico, aimed at the customers at the bottom of the pyramid and is now expanding and monitoring its market by associating social networks. The company expanded its business in the United States and other countries in Latin America. It is operating as an innovative project aimed at meeting the needs of the families of relative lower socio-demographic profile (Drayton and Budinich 2010).

Social Business Designs: Co-creation and Coevolution

Social business is a value-led function involving customers, stakeholders, and entrepreneurs. The initiatives of involving the social entities in co-creating products and services help companies in driving quickly to social business due to wider acceptability among customers. Social businesses are more effective in outreaching bottom-of-the pyramid customer segment and transforming demand for innovative products. Therefore, building social base for innovative products ensures reaping of higher gains as compared to the market-oriented competitive strategies. Co-creation is an upcoming phenomenon in business ecosystem, which involves society and business in sharing and adapting experiences of people respectively. It is a bi-directional dynamic of exchanging ideas, experiences, innovation concepts, developing prototypes, and commercializing generic thought into the business avenues. Experience co-creation is an art, which is portrayed by the business communities with the support of personal and digital interfaces to know the insights of all players in market operations including customers. Co-creating business models with the underlying customer and stakeholder experiences has emerged as a new paradigm of strategy innovation. Customer-centric companies like Nestlé, Conagra, Amazon, Unilever, and Tata India are able to explore the public domain holistically today to innovate products and services with compelling value propositions through co-creating strategy with effective employee engagement (e.g. Ramaswamy and Gouillart 2008).

Social media channels have given enormous opportunity to the companies to interact with the customers, social activists, sociocultural leaders, and entrepreneurs. The overwhelming response of people to the social networking, from Facebook and Twitter to YouTube video manifestations and to the informal community blogs, endorses co-creation as an effective strategy-building tool, which integrates public views to reconstruct businesses for the customers and by the customers. Co-creation is increasingly employed in production and marketing operations by the social innovation companies, who reorient their business strategies by analyzing the active and passive experiences of customers and stakeholders. Multinational companies have focused on building corporate social reputation by co-creating brand experiences embedding customer knowledge and consumption practices as an internal power of the organization. Such practices emphasize continuous interchange of ideas, involvement of customers, stakeholders, and supplier, social influence on business, and corporate openness to the co-creation (Ramaswamy 2009).

The competition attracts the firms seeking to capitalize on an available business opportunity. As the number of firms get involved in the process of sharing the pie, the degree of competition increases. When the entire market represents one large homogeneous unit, the intensity of competition is much greater than segmented market However, if a market is not appropriate for segmentation, firms may compete to serve it homogeneously, thus intensifying competition (Zook and Allen 2003). Hence, in either of the market situation the intensity of competition is unavoidable for the participating firms. Understanding the co-creation and coevolution (C&C) of the rival, and developing the company's own, are the most important tasks in sailing through the marketing competition. In managing the convergence of societal needs and business goals, the major challenge faced by the companies is to analyze the visible and subconscious emotions of customers, which are often translucent and mislead the co-creation and coevolution process. Consequently, connecting the dots between subconscious insights, experience and visible emotions to co-creation innovations, and develop business models is not a consistent process. The conscious and subconscious thought processes are two different processes, and need to be treated independently in co-creation and coevolution processes. In so doing, making sense of visible emotions and subconscious thoughts appears to be the major challenge in building customer-centric and socially responsible business models. Nonetheless, the precision in analyzing the variations of thoughts in conscious and subconscious states of mind of customers, which can sharpen knowledge about consumer behavior and improve co-creation and coevolution marketing practices.

Co-creation and coevolution are essential practices for winning the market place, and sustaining and getting the competitive leverage. The capabilities in general address as how well an organization performs or executes some of the vital activities like customer relationship management, and services and supply chain management etc. Competency may be stated as what an organization does well across the region and subsidiary units or customer segments. In all, the C&C involve action, the focus, and emphasis on what the competitor does in the market to outperform its business rival. There are many attributes of C&C, however, the following may be defined as the key attributes of the C&C:

- Dynamism in ideation and thought process
- Span of effects on social business models
- Robustness in psychosocial analysis of information
- Limitations and ability to expand

Dynamism of the C&C refers to the continuous change for the betterment of the corporate social policies and execution of the strategies. Companies must be able to coevolve continuously in new markets and avoid being static in exploring customer emotions and experiences to manage co-creation and coevolution. Companies with social business modeling can narrow down the emotional and though process discrepancies by analyzing the customer though process over spatial and temporal dimensions.

Single-factor innovations tap one competence, and capable competitors can usually match it. Multiple competences strengthen several dimensions and in effect redefine the basis of competition. The *shadow strategy task force* is offered as a method to force managers to relinquish the comfort of the firm's accepted view of itself. This approach begins with the objective of identifying the strategies and competence that, in the hands of competitors, might be used to attack the firm's competitive position successfully. Especially critical on the task force are individuals with insight into how customers, suppliers, and competitors view the firm's products and services. Developing new competence requires constant experimentation. The innovation–imitation–equilibrium cycle suggests that industry leaders teach customers what to demand by defining the current state of the art in performance, price, service, and other dimensions; customers learn to judge competitive offerings against these standards, and the learning effect is cumulative (Werther and Kerr 1995). However, involving customers in co-creation process raises their expectations along various dimensions of marketing mix (comprising product, price, place, promotion, performance, and psychodynamics), and the intensity and extent of participation in future co-creation projects. Motivation among customers plays a significant role in driving their participation in the co-creation and coevolution of business models. The stimulations to customers' participation in these projects include monetary reward (e.g.. Google survey rewards), recognition, challenges, and social awards (contents and social events), upholding intrinsic interest, and inculcating curiosity. Such motivations encourage customers to explain different customer expectations. Participants also vary in their personal characteristics and expectations toward virtual co-creation (Fuller 2010). The ecosystem of social business modeling, which describes the attributes of co-creation and coevolution is illustrated in Figure 3.2.

The social business design has six broad constituents comprising co-creation, coevolution, psychosocial drivers, corporate policies, and intrinsic and extrinsic factors as exhibited in Figure 3.2. Companies working with the concept of co-creation focus on managing shared information and inducing creative thinking to develop social innovation. Co-creation is aimed at providing new solutions to meet social problems and create intrinsic and extrinsic values through experience sharing. Successful co-creation of innovations comes with a major challenge of commercialization, which has driven the co-created products and services to evolve ambidextrously with society and corporations. Employee engagement and customer

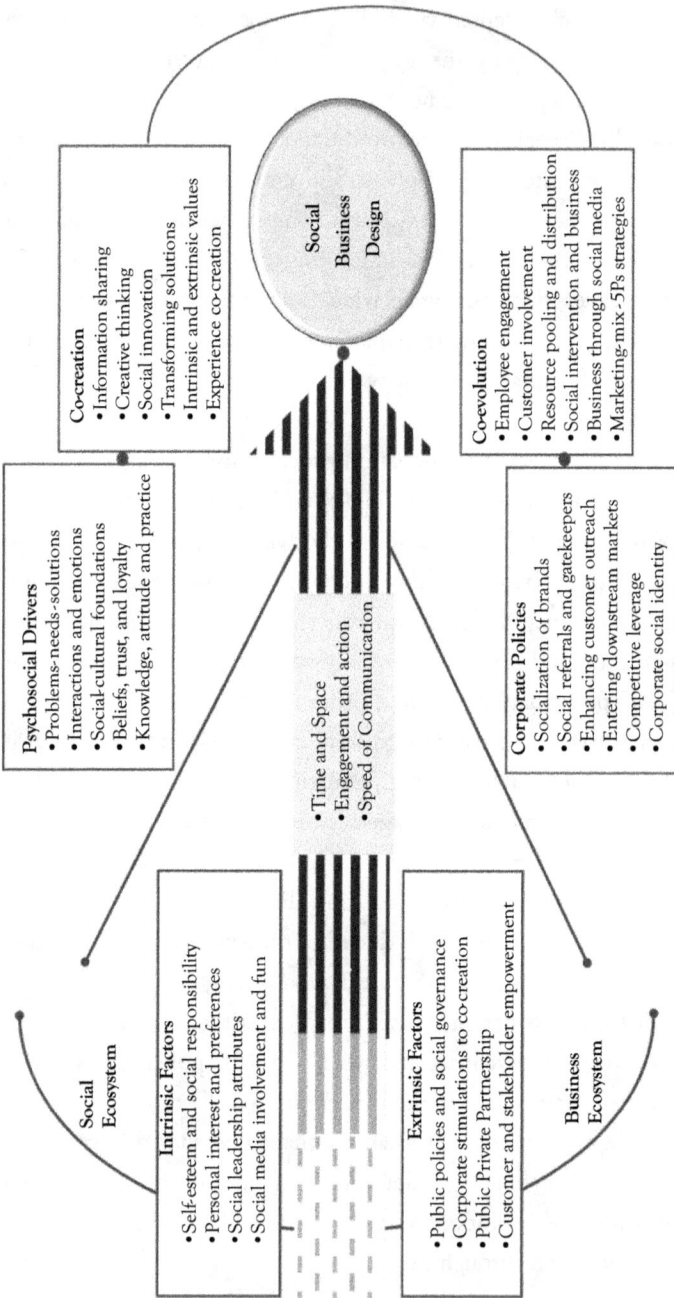

Figure 3.2 Ecosystem of social business modeling

Source: Author.

involvement are the pillars of coevolution process, beside resource pool-ing, distribution, and managing marketing mix (product, price, place, pro-motion, and psychodynamics) functions. Social business design is largely based on the psychosocial drivers that affect co-creation of innovations and strategies, and the commercialization process. Customer and stake-holder participation in co-creating innovation and marketing strategies co-creation is effective in exploring the solutions to social problems and determining the needs. Participation in a social purpose is be interactive and emotional as compared to the involvement of customers and stake-holders in an absolute commercial project. The social, cultural, and ethnic foundations nurture belief, trust, and loyalty perceptions during the col-lective efforts in innovation and developing marketing strategies. Com-panies carrying out the co-creation process gain societal insights from the knowledge, attitude, and practices (conventional of intermediate) toward finding the social solutions. Most social entrepreneurs join co-creation projects and set mutual benefit goals with the business corporations. In addition, the companies benefit by co-creation process in socializing their existing and upcoming brands by developing referrals and brand gatekeepers in the societal niche, which helps in enhancing the customer outreach. Societal engagement of business corporations opens avenues to enter the downstream markets alongside the mass and premium market segments, driving them to conquer the universe of market (comprising premium, upper mass, regular mass, lower mass, and bottom-of-the-pyr-amid market segment). In an interactive social and business environment, coevolution of businesses with the societal values provides competitive leverage to the companies and help in achieving corporate social identity. The intrinsic factors within the social ecosystem that stimulate the co-cre-ation process of social entrepreneurs, customers, and stakeholders include social responsibility led self-esteem, voluntary behavior, social leadership, and active involvement in social media. The extrinsic factors of business ecosystem that attract co-creation and coevolution process with social stakeholders comprise social governance, public policies, public–private partnership, and the leverage of empowering social stakeholders toward promoting the social businesses.

Developing co-created innovations and commercializing them have two distinct challenges. Marketing co-created brands have com-monly slow organic growth within the organization and target markets.

However, the companies need to develop competence in marketing co-created and coevolved innovation products by establishing social values consistently. There are many ways to categorize core competence. However, these may be broadly distinguished as market access competence, integrity-related competence and to functionality-related competence. The market access competence includes management of brand development, sales and marketing, distribution and logistics, and technical support. All these skills help to put a firm in close proximity to its customers. The attributes associated with competence like quality, cycle time management, just-in-time inventory management, and so on, which allow a company to do things more quickly, flexibly or with a higher degree of reliability than competitors constitute the integrity-related competence of a firm. The functionality-related competence leads toward improving the skills, which enable the company to invest in its services or products with unique functionality. Such competence drive companies toward capitalizing the products and services with distinctive customer benefits, rather than merely making it incrementally better. The functionality-related competence is becoming more important as a source of competitive differentiation, relative to the other two competence types.

Social marketing and social business designs are surviving since decades as companies try to inculcate consumption behavior among the lower mass and bottom-of-the-pyramid market segments for the commercial brands. Nestlé used social marketing to market its baby food products (milk powder, cereal brands including *Cerelac* and *Nestum*, and recently acquired Gerber brand). The company has planned programs to encourage co-creation of user-generated contents for advertisements, ideas for campaigns, and voluntary participation for health education at prenatal, natal, and lactating stages of mother and child care. Such corporate moves have stimulated nongovernmental organizations (NGOs) and community self-help groups toward learning to cooperate with each other. Realizing the benefits associated with the socialization of brands, the corporate performance is built within business–society and market domains. Accordingly, companies are working together with the society to co-create innovative business models and help in growing new markets at the bottom-of-the-pyramid segments and enhance the outreach of customers. The path to convergence has proceeded through the following stages (e.g. Brugmann and Prahalad 2007):

- Identifying mutual interests between the society and companies, and coevolving collaborative projects linking social needs and corporate responsibilities
- Managing coexistence of social and corporate stakes in innovations, strategy development, and market operations
- Sharing experience and social thoughts to empower customers as change agents and business promoters within the broad areas of social interests
- Learning business disciplines of business houses by the social stakeholders vis-à-vis companies to understand the social and cultural needs, culture, and values, and
- Developing local knowledge, low-cost business models, and community-based marketing techniques to co-create social business models and implement community-led marketing approaches.

In the growing competitive phenomenon, the companies are converging around universally high standards for product and service integrity, and are moving through alliances, acquisitions, and industry consolidation to build broadly matching global brand and distribution capabilities. Interestingly, the Japanese concept of quality has shifted from an idea centered on integrity (*zero defects*) to one focused on functionality (*quality that surprises* in that the product yields a unique functionality benefit to the customer). Comparative analysis examines the specific advantages of competitors within a given market and offers structural and response advantages. Structural advantages are those built into the business, for example, a manufacturing plant in Mexico may, because of low labor costs, have a built-in advantage over another firm. Responsive advantages refer to positions of comparative advantage that have accrued to a business over time as a result of certain decisions. This type of advantage is based on leveraging the strategic phenomena at work in the business. Besides, the examination of the business system operating in an industry is useful in analyzing competitors and in searching out innovative options for gaining a sustainable competitive advantage. The framework may also be used to analyze a competitor's costs and to gain insights into the sources of a competitor's current advantage in either cost or economic value to the customer.

The price of engaging in these social network activities includes the monetary costs for the network group participants, who may be considered as profit-linked promotion of the health care company and drive the debate against the company by a radical group. The network manager of the company needs to streamline this debate on the right track and filter the unrelated conversation. Promotion could be done by the health care company through public service announcements, billboards, mass mailings, media events and community outreach. Accordingly, partnerships could be cultivated with social networks online along with exclusive women's groups, corporate sponsors, medical organizations, and service clubs and media outlets to drive the equilibrium in the thought process and convey the corporate goals to the target audience. Some other possible allies to cultivate are physicians, insurance companies, and the local cancer society. The company may deploy each element of the marketing mix as the core marketing strategy.

Summary

Social engagement is manifested discretely in the corporate culture, organizational behavior, and functional practices of companies. In order to create and measure the impact of business models, the collaborative approaches of customers and stakeholders in business ecosystem works effectively in socializing the businesses. The business outcomes ultimately percolate down to the social stream and companies tend to get a public applause or criticism during the social appraisals. The factors of knowing, doing, and being form the core of design-to-society approach. Investing in design-to-society programs to inculcate social values in brand without appropriate design-to-market approaches might reduce the expected growth, profits, and business expansion of companies. The design-to-society approach is founded on the value-based business thinking, which explains the "competing with social purpose" and "performance with purpose" concepts underlying in the welfare marketing business school of thought. Co-creation is continuous process of collaborative efforts between society, customers, stakeholders, and the company. Optimal collaborations focus on new product development through frugal or incremental innovations, and improving business processes market performance. The design-to-society attributes are transforming today from conventional wisdom to the digital tools to socialize brands and deliver social values. The digital interactions among customers help companies socialize brands and create brand value for competitive leverage. Socialization of marketing strategies, innovations, and brands drive collective impact among customers, which strengthens the competitive positions of companies in the marketplace.

Business and society convergence is supported by the transformational and transactional thinking by co-creating solutions to the societal problems related to business sector. The social marketing strategies have appeared as an effective tool to align business goals with the social development and value generation perspectives. Effective social networking on digital and face-to-face interactions enable companies to design network marketing. Engaging customers in marketing process drives psychodynamics and enhances the scope of peer brand building. Social marketing platforms have increasingly involved customers not only in communication, but also in designing the social websites of companies. The active roles of stakeholders in community interactions and experiences sharing have helped companies in co-creating products and services, and user-generated marketing content to enhance the market competitiveness of their products and services. Customer-centric companies develop social marketing programs and campaigns to reach customers to create awareness on brands, promote brands at the competitive edge, and enhance their brand experience on real time. Design-to-society approach to targeted community provides a significant benefit to the customers and stakeholders over the conventional for-profit marketing methods. The most effective programs use a combination of mass media, community, small group and individual activities. When a simple, clear message is repeated in many places and formats throughout the community, it is more likely to be seen and remembered.

Understanding social needs is an essential challenge for the companies to create social value by delivering right solutions. In order to dive deep into the social needs, communication is critical to explore the social cognition and construct strategic or tactical solutions. Brand communities have grown along the corporate site for sharing experiences of variety-seeking customers in the context of value-based activities. The communally seeded and empowered customers are now a marketplace reality as they portray social needs, preferences, and values on the business canvas. Most companies involve social networks and social media in managing the social projects as communication interface. Such social platforms are very effective in socializing the corporate brands. Social business is a value-led function involving customers, stakeholders, and entrepreneurs. The initiatives of involving the social entities in co-creating products and services help companies in driving quickly to social business due to wider acceptability among customers. Companies working with the concept of co-creation focus on managing shared information and inducing creative thinking to develop social innovation. Co-creation is aimed at providing new solution to meet social problems and create intrinsic and extrinsic values through experience sharing to help transforming solutions. Successful co-creation of innovations comes with a major challenge of commercialization, which has driven the co-created products and services to evolve ambidextrously with society and corporations. In an interactive social and business environment, coevolution of businesses with the societal values provides competitive leverage to the companies and help in achieving corporal social identity.

References

Armelini, G., and J. Villanueva. 2011. "Adding Social Media to the Marketing-Mix." *IESE-Insight Magazine* 3, no. 4, pp. 29–36.

Berger, I.E., P.H. Cunningham, and M.E. Drumwright. 2004. "Social Alliances: Company/Nonprofit Collaboration." *California Management Review* 47, no. 1, pp. 58–90.

Brugmann, J., and C.K. Prahalad. 2007. "Co-creating Business's New Social Compact." *Harvard Business Review* 85, no. 2, pp. 80–90.

Bloom, P.N., and A. Chatterji. 2009. "Scaling Social Entrepreneurial Impact." *California Management Review* 51, no. 3, pp. 114–133.

Conklin, J., and K. Christensen. Winter 2009. "Building Shared Understanding of Wicked Problems - Interview with Jeff Conklin." *Rotman Magazine*.

Cross, R., S.P. Borgatti, and A. Parkar. 2002. "Making Invisible Work Visible: Using Social Network Analysis to Support Strategic Collaboration." *California Management Review* 44, no. 2, pp. 25–46.

Cross, R., J.M. Liedtka, and L. Weiss. 2005. "Practical Guide to Social Networks." *Harvard Business Review* 83, no. 3, pp. 124–132.

Calefato, F., and F. Lanubile. 2010. "Communication Media Selection for Remote Interaction of Ad Hoc Groups." In *Advances in Computers*, Vol. 78, 271–313. Elsevier.

Drayton, B., and V. Budinich. 2010. "A New Alliance for Global Change." *Harvard Business Review* 88, no. 9, pp. 56–64.

Dyer, J.H., P. Kale, and H. Singh. 2001. "How to Make Strategic Alliances Work." *Sloan Management Review* 42, no. 4, pp. 37–43.

Fleming, L., and M. Marx. 2006. "Managing Creativity in the Small Worlds." *California Management Review* 48, no. 4, pp. 6–27.

Fuller, J. 2010. "Refining Virtual Co-Creation from a Customer Perspective." *California Management Review* 52, no. 2, pp. 98–122.

Gamboa, A.M., and H.M. Goncalves. 2014. "Customer Loyalty through Social Networks: Lessons from Zara on Facebook." *Business Horizons* 57, no. 6, pp. 709–717.

Hanna, R.C., A. Rohm, and V.L. Crittenden. 2011. "We're all Connected: The Power of the Social Media Ecosystem." *Business Horizons* 54, no. 3, pp. 265–273.

Hutt, M.D., E.R. Stafford, B.A. Walker, and P.H. Reingen. 2000. "Defining the Social Network of a Strategic Alliance." *Sloan Management Review* 41, no. 2, pp. 51–62.

Kane, G.C., R.G. Fichman, J. Gallaugher, and J. Glaser. 2009. "Community Relations 2.0." *Harvard Business Review* 87, no. 11, pp. 45–50.

Kaplan, A.M. 2012. "If you Love Something, Let it Go Mobile: Mobile Marketing and Mobile Social Media 4x4." *Business Horizons* 55, no. 2, pp. 129–139.

Kramer, M.R., and M. Pfitzer. 2016. "The Ecosystem of Shared Value." *Harvard Business Review* 94, no. 10, pp. 80–89.

Millar, L.G. and N.A. Christakis. 2011. "Tapping the Power of Social Networks." *Harvard Business Review* 89, no. 9, pp. 28–29.

Muñiz, A.M., and H.J. Schau. 2011. "How to Inspire Value-Laden Collaborative Customer-Generated Content." *Business Horizons* 54, no. 3, pp. 209–217.

Nidumolu, R., J. Ellison, J. Whalen, and E. Billman. 2014. "The Collaboration Imperative." *Harvard Business Review* 92, no. 4, pp. 76–84.

Paniagua, J., and J. Sapena. 2014. "Business Performance and Social Media: Love or Hate?" *Business Horizons* 57, no. 6, pp. 719–728.

Piskorski, M.J. 2011. "Social Strategies that Work." *Harvard Business Review* 89, no. 11, pp. 116–122.

Porter, M.E. and J. Heppelmann. 2014. "How Smart, Connected Products Are Transforming Competition." *Harvard Business Review* 92, no. 11, pp. 64–88.

Porter, M.E., and M.R. Kramer. 2006. "Strategy and Society: The Link Between Competitive Advantage and Corporate Social Responsibility." *Harvard Business Review* 84, no. 12, pp. 78–92.

Rajagopal. 2013. *Managing Social Media and Consumerism: The Grapevine Effect in Competitive Markets.* Basingstoke, UK: Palgrave Macmillan.

Ramaswamy, V. 2009. "Are You Ready for the Co-Creation Movement?" *IESE-Insight Magazine* Third Quarter, no. 2, pp. 29–35.

Ramaswamy, V., and F.J. Gouillart. 2008. *Co-Creating Strategy with Experience Co-Creation.* Harvard Business School News Letter, Cambridge: Harvard Business School Press.

Rangan, V.K., S. Karim, and S.K. Sandberg. 1996. "Do Better at Doing Good." *Harvard Business Review* 74, no. 3, pp. 42–54.

Rodriguez-Vila, O., and S. Bharadwaj. September- October, 2017. "Competing on Social Purpose." *Harvard Business Review*, pp. 94–101.

Spenner, P. 2010. "Why you Need a New-Media Ringmaster." *Harvard Business Review* 88, no. 12, pp. 78–79.

Ustuner, T., and D.B. Godes. 2006. "Better Sales Networks." *Harvard Business Review* 84, no. 7, pp. 102–112.

Vargo, S.L., and R.F. Lusch. 2004. "Evolving to a New Dominant Logic for Marketing." *Journal of Marketing* 68, no. 1, pp. 1–17.

Werther, W.B., and J.L. Kerr. 1995. "The Shifting Sands of Competitive Advantage." *Business Horizons* 38, no. 3, pp. 11–17.

Wheeler, D., K. McKague, J. Thomson, R. Davies, J. Medalye, and M. Prada. 2005. "Creating Sustainable Local Enterprise Networks." *Sloan Management Review* 47, no. 1, pp. 33–40.

Zook, C., and J. Allen. 2003. "Growth Outside the Core." *Harvard Business Review* 81, no. 12, pp. 66–73.

CHAPTER 4

Design-to-Value

Overview

Customer value contributes significantly to the business performance of a company. Most companies today focus on creating value in collaboration with customers within the synchronized socio-business ecosystems. The design-to-value philosophy is streamlined with the design-to-society and design-to-market concepts. In the strategy pyramid of the firm, society and business constitute the foundation elements, while the value is projected on the top of the pyramid. This chapter discusses comprehensively the attributes toward understanding customers to lay the foundation for design-to-value marketing modeling. The arguments supporting the design-to-value models are discussed in the context of cognitive values, psychological attributes, and the underlying business philosophy of firms. Discussions on perceptual semantics, as an interconnected thought process of customers driven by the collective knowledges and personality attributes, also support the arguments on design-to-value concept. The chapter also discusses behavioral determinants in the context of creating customer lifetime value.

Understanding Customers

Customer behavior is a dynamic cognition process. Customer behavior and customerism are contextual to social and cultural ecosystems besides the economic and market leverages. Customer psychology, perceptual dimensions, and cognitive ergonomics are highly complex, and a small part has been discovered so far in the wide array of research studies so far. The common business touchpoints to understand customers are knowledge, self-reference, motivations, social and economic benefits, and collective intelligence on value structures. Customer behavior can be explained with the attributes of social cognitive theory, which argues that self-regulation and self-efficacy guide the buying behavior and develop social-personal congruence in cognitive thought process. Behavioral attributes influence customer perceptions toward the contextual, sociocultural and personal relevance of a product or service, which contribute to the lifestyle, values, and deriving satisfaction. The lifestyle theory suggests that the customers' perceived hedonic attributes and social identity factors determine the shopping behavior of urban customers. This theory explains customer behavior toward construction of social and self-identity, creating values, and deriving utilitarian or hedonic pleasure by engagement in lifestyle practices. The lifestyle perceptions contribute significantly toward the making buying decisions amidst the competitive brands and services, and changing consumption practices.

Value perceptions among customers are induced by the social, economic, and relational factors. The social learning theory explains this phenomenon as a positive reinforcement, and it occurs when a behavior (response) is followed by a favorable stimulus (commonly seen as pleasant) that increases the frequency of that behavior. In the conceptual foundations of social learning theory, respondent conditioning and observational learning are empirically supported approaches to understanding the normative human development and the etiology of psychosocial problems. Social learning process is widely influenced by the manifold growth of social media, digital networks, and interpersonal communications. Information technology has dramatically changed the social communication inflow by the customers sharing experiences, values, new product ideas, and complaints about companies and products. Online customer reviews extend word-of-mouth from new acquaintances and transform information from personal to public channels on social media platforms where interactions among experienced customers occur (Pfeffer et al. 2014).

Social learning process is oriented to individual's cognition and is beyond the socioeconomic profile of people. However, the geo-demographic explosion of middle-income social segment comprising all types of customers. Gender polarization of customers in the marketplace has significantly affected the social value systems and lifestyle practices. Besides, urbanization, income inequality in the society, growing millennial trends, and the shrinking corporate values have been the major factors influencing radical shifts in customer behavior. In addition, the attributes that stimulate experimentation and drive changes in the consumption patterns increase as the manufacturing companies and retailers enhance shopping conveniences like credit transactions, self-service return policies, and competitive promotions, besides focus on wellness and green consumption. Customer behavior in the competitive marketplace is widely influenced by the discretionary spending, buying low-cost products, and gaining value for money. Companies practicing incremental marketing technologies are able to understand the dynamics of customer preferences by using digital data analytics, social media-driven consumption patterns, and customer experience through virtual reality. Shopping value built through the shopping experiences is one of the key indicators that influence consumption ecosystem. The personal shopping value is determined through multiple behavioral constructs including satisfaction, pleasure-arousal-dominance in visual merchandising and touch-feel-pick cognitive synchronization, word-of-mouth, social value and lifestyle, and corporate patronage (Jones et al. 2006).

Value perceptions among customers with utilitarian perspectives reflect rational, instrumental, and task-related consumption, while hedonic dimensions correspond to affective, emotional, and luxury values and lifestyle. Visual appeal of the product and services no longer attracts the customer to make a purchase decision. They buy experiences and emotions which a brand can offer. Digitalization of markets has trained customers to expect continuous excitement and value additions to their experiences. Growth of e-commerce alongside the brick-and-mortar retail stores has encouraged customers to expand their experience with different types of channels. Consequently, the value spread of the shopping experiences of customers has run through the vertical channel (single channel performance with incremental growth over time) to horizontal channels (across the virtual and omni-channel experience) within rapidly expanding competitive marketplaces. The customer value is increasingly delivered through the embedded servitization beyond the boundaries of physical channels, which is clearly distinguishable in creating customer experience. In order to enhance the design-to-value experience with the customers, companies today focus on providing multiple shopping experience than engaging in a single shopping channel. This value-driven marketing strategy is compatible with the design cube concept, wherein companies converge design-to-market strategies with design-to-society and design-to-value strategies. Such convergence enhances multiple experiences across channels that culminate in a seamless and comprehensive customer-value journey (Verhoef, Kannan, and Inman 2015; Treadgold and Reynolds 2016). Therefore, the rapid shifts in the customer behavior have become noticeable as the conventional value propositions are outpacing growth among the technology-oriented customers in the global emerging markets.

Consumption activities are driven by the lifestyle goals and sustain if they satisfy the basic needs and provide social and personal distinctions in using the product and services. Customers are often interested in higher satisfaction by consuming innovative and socially differentiated products to achieve self-realization, fairness, freedom, participation, social relations, and balance among the consumption ecosystem. Such customer aspirations may be served either by unique selling proposition, self-esteem, and corporate image, or by new generation products launched by the companies. For many customers, consumption defines a significant part of their role in the society, as sharing experience about products among peers helps in creating and maintaining relationships. It may be a basis for self-respect and a significant part of what gives life interest and meaning. Customerism has emerged historically across the changing market environment and has created mass markets, industrialization, and cultural attitudes that ensure that rising incomes are used to purchase an ever-growing output (Sharpe and Staelin 2010).

Consumption has often been dichotomized in terms of its functional-hedonic nature and is closely associated with the level of satisfaction leading to determine the customer value influence (Wakefield and Inman 2003). As the new products are introduced, a firm may routinely pass these costs on to customers, resulting in high prices. However, a less obvious strategy in a competitive situation may be to maintain price, in order to drive the new product in the market with more emphasis on quality, brand name, postsales services and customer relations management as nonprice factors. Studies that advocate the models of building customer value through traditional relationship marketing discuss the long-term value concepts to loyal customers. Most importantly, the approaches suggested in these studies are expected to rise their spending and association with the products and services of the company with increasing levels of customer satisfaction (Reichheld and Sasser 1990). In a marketing environment of a firm, brand should be grown by studying the conditions under which it is expected to sustain. The various factors which affect the management of a brand includes:

- Social and cultural factors
- Market competition related factors
- Customer perceptions
- Economic factors related to business and customer

Customer perceptions are often agile and need to be endorsed by the peers, friends, and family to support decision making and to put them into practice over a long term. Such cognitive process creates consumption attitude among customers. Perceptions linked to emotions are commonly impulsive and temporary, which do not make a dent on cognitive process continuity and help in decision making. The perceptions should be measurable. Customers generally measure their perceived values in reference to the desired satisfaction in terms of value for money derived through the convergence of quality and price. Higher perceived value of customers not only justifies the quality of the perceptual process among customers but also determines the social leadership by way of how many follow a right perception of a customer as referral. Perceptions of customers should also be able to analyze the right information at the right time and distinguish the attributes of personal and social determinants that influence the cognitive process. Customer perceptions constitute 4Rs that determine the cognitive process and validate the perceived notion on products and services comprising *recognize, review, reflect*, and *reconstruct*. *Recognize* factor explains that customers form perceptions on the viable solutions to the predetermined needs (recognized as problems), which match with their self-congruence and could offer sustainable value (satisfaction). Customers *review* their perceptions formed on product, services, brands, or business companies in reference to the public opinions and own observations. Accordingly, customers justify their perceptions and develop purchase intentions. *Reflect*, as a perceptual indicator, explains self-validation of the decision taken. Upon developing the right perceptions, customers try to refine their needs and find means and ends to acquire the product. Consumption of products establishes the perceived value among customers and validates their buying decision. Perceptions initially formed by the customers are often subject to change in view of the reviews, referrals, and self-reflections. Perceptions are reconstituted accordingly by moving to new market ambiance, by brands with new attributes, and by redefining the need. Accordingly, new perceptual criteria are set by the customers to pursue their needs. This cognitive state explains the *reconstruction* of perceptions. Therefore, companies need to understand the factors that drive customer stimuli toward getting associated with new products and brands. The cognitive drivers that affect customer behavior are discussed as follows:

- Acquiring social status by changing the consumption pattern
- Achieving self-esteem and personality enhancement
- Satisfying hedonic value and self-governance, and
- Staying in public domain and gaining social prominence

These factors help companies develop customer behavior and manage the related business environments to develop marketing strategy and inculcate customer behavior. An understanding of the environment helps managers assess the extent of the investment required to strengthen the brand, and develop strategies accordingly. Conditions of brand environment provide a base for formulating the brand policy and its measurement to provide magnitude and direction categorically to the brands of a company.

Design-to-Value Marketing Modeling

Customer value-led marketing modeling is an outgrowth of design-to-market philosophy, which companies are increasingly focusing on to polarize customers in competitive markets and build consistent value-base to acquire and retain customers. Such strategy has helped most companies reduce the incidence of customer defection from one brand to another. Creating customer value has, therefore, become the contemporary benchmark to measure market performance of a company and building design-to-value based businesses. The customer value propositions resonate in marketing models to lead the business by putting the customer first. Such marketing philosophy has enabled large companies like PepsiCo to conceptualize and implement the business strategy of performance with purpose. Co-created customer values help companies focus on customer-centric product offerings to gain competitive advantage. Upon understanding the perceptions, emotions, and values of customers, companies make smarter choices about allocation of resources in customer services, advertisement and communications, and implementation of marketing-mix driven strategies. The co-created and coevolved customer value constructs are able to deliver optimal benefits to customers by upholding their perceptions, choices, and self-esteem. The actualization of customer values often needs social validation as customer perceptions largely evolve around social learning. There is often a close match of customer self-image congruence and social cognition, as these factors play significant role in moderating their buying decisions. Firms can provide a simple and powerful customer value propositions by making their offerings superior on the few elements that matter most to the target customers. Such strategy helps firms in creating the customer value and communicating to the customer communities to provide better understanding on the business priorities of customers (Anderson et al. 2006).

It is often difficult to fully explore the behavior of customers as there remains many unidentified perceptions and subconscious emotions. Companies sometimes make quick behavioral assessment of customers to develop short-term marketing decisions without understanding the longer-term implications for their customer base. However, most emerging enterprises overspend in creating customer value without understanding the perceptions, emotions, and behavioral attributes of customers. Consequently, such companies end up with low-value customers or pursuing activities that have little influence on customer behavior. Large companies with strategies focus on customers develop value dashboard to monitor customer touchpoints, which helps in co-creating customer value proposition. A good customer value dashboard helps firms not only in increasing sales and marketing professionals but also in developing design-to-society and design-to-value business modeling (Villanueva 2013).

It has been observed that cultural values affect the purchase intentions of customers across the market segments. In the societies that exhibit hedonic values, fashion apparel is promoted by manufacturers and retailers to induce a sudden, compelling, socially complex buying behavior through promotional programs, to increase their disposable income by facilitating credit to customer (Venkatesh et al. 2010). Manufacturers and retailers apply both push and pull strategies to make the promotions of brands effective and advantageous to the customers. Promotions targeted at final customers, known as pull promotions, directly offer extra value to customers, with the primary goals of attracting customers to retail locations, and stimulating immediate sales. Though both push and pull promotions are designed to speed up the selling process and increase sales at least in the short term, their strategic implications as well as their impacts on product sales and profits are believed to be different. Such promotion-led retailing culture stimulates fashion-oriented attitudes, debt, and spending behavior on clothing, among customers (Martin-Herran et al. 2010).

Social and cultural values influence customers' personal values and alter cognitive dynamics comprising attention, semantics, memory, perception, problem-solving abilities, creativity, conscious thinking, and decision rationale. The cognitive value assessments are a major task in understanding the underlying personal, social, and cultural values among customers in the conscious and subconscious states of mind. Commonly, customer value models are built by analyzing the psychosocial data on key decision indicators with the spatial and temporal dimensions. However, these assessments are not definitive as they change rapidly over time, space, and preferences, and within a given social ambiance. The value model for an individual customer or for a community within the market segment can be constructed drawing collective intelligence (psychosocial and cultural information) inferences. The design-to-value models are largely indicative to the firms, which guide in create competitive advantage by creating customer values and augment market competitiveness in several ways as discussed as follows (Anderson and Narus 1999):

- Co-created customer value provides opportunity to the firms on capitalizing on the dynamic preferences, perceptions, measures of satisfaction, and loyalty standpoints

- Monitoring inevitable variation in customers' needs and planning for flexible market offerings, demonstrating the customer value models toward developing new product or service with predetermined performance benchmarks
- Using the tacit knowledge of customers in developing design-to-market strategy to deliver value-based market offers
- Coevolving business models through persuasive value propositions and gain market competitiveness by putting the customer first
- Using design-to-value models to provide evidence to customers of their accomplishments and sharing their experience on social media channels to acquire new customers though the induced psychodynamics (brand pull effect).

Firms realize the benefits by measuring and monitoring the cognitive determinants of customers and reinforcing the business philosophy for the customers and by the customers by delivering desired values to customers. Such strategy complies with the attributes of the design-to-value, design-to-society, and design-to-market business design cube. The value-creation path in design-to-value based business modeling is depicted in Figure 4.1.

The path of design-to-value modeling is based on customer cognition, psychosocial attributes, and business philosophy of market governance in the firms as illustrated in Figure 4.1. The value creation is a derivation of conscious cognition, actions in subconscious mind, unconscious perceptions, and materialistic reasoning. The cognitive ergonomics of customers (emotions, perceptions, and memories and storyboards), knowledge, beliefs, and trust, and the abilities of information analysis constitute the conscious cognition, which embeds customer value perceptions. Customer values are also affected by unaffordable desires, social comparisons triggering inferiority feelings, and the need for socioeconomic equity. These attributes evolve in the subconscious mind of customers, while the value destructions and transitions occur unconsciously in the minds of customers. Such state of mind often causes cognitive delusions and unearths implicit memories in conjunction with unconscious thought process, which is difficult to trace and portray on

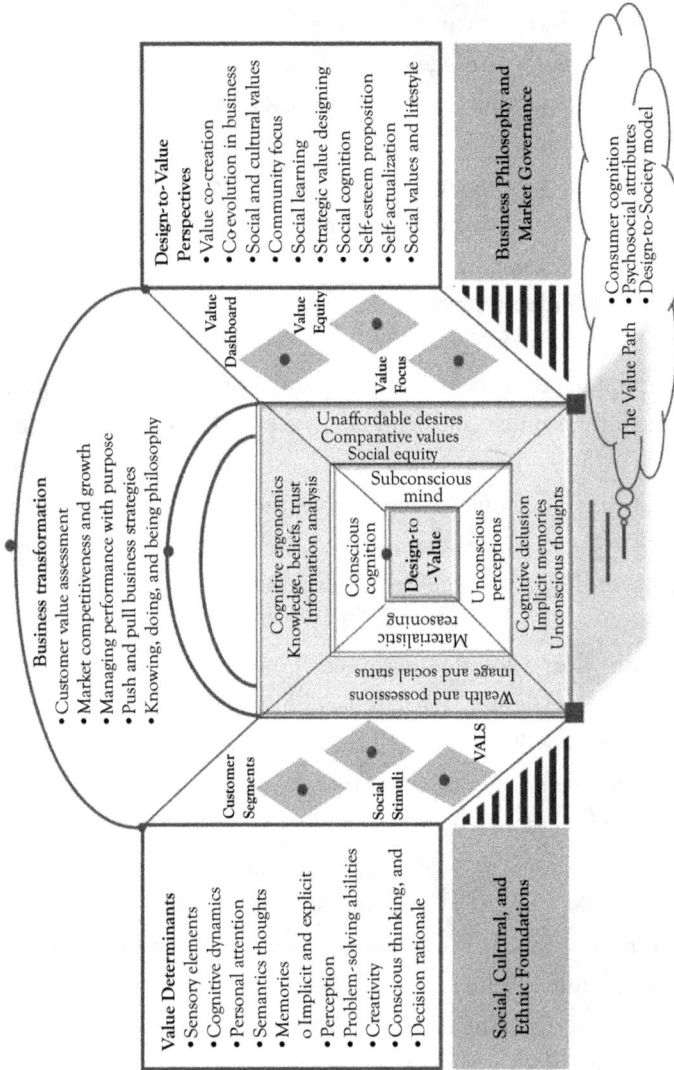

Figure 4.1 *The value path in design-to-value business modeling.*

Source: Author.

the value canvas. However, customers have materialistic desire toward accumulating wealth and possession of products to determine unique image and social value propositions. In context of the earlier discussion, determinants of the value path are constructed through the customer cognition process, psychosocial attributes, and business modeling based on the design-to-society philosophy. Periodical assessment of customer value being intangible and transitionary, companies are able to develop market competitive strategies to stimulate business growth. Companies following the design-to-value philosophy tend to put customers first in building and implementing competitive marketing strategies comprising push (resource-based marketing approach with all elements of marketing mix) and pull (psychodynamics and nonzero-sum game) approaches. Customer value-centric companies usually engage in knowing (exploring value perceptions), doing (implementing pro-customer strategies), and being (enjoying the state of win-win by serving the customers), which enables them to achieve performance with purpose.

Figure 4.1 illustrates broad value determinants that envelop sensory elements and needs for personal attention, problem-solving abilities, creativity, and conscious thinking. These determinants contribute to the cognitive dynamics, which are enhanced by the semantic (interconnected and value-led) thoughts, implicit and explicit memories, and value-driven perceptions. In the corporate context, the design-to-value perspectives include co-creation of customer value and coevolving business by engaging customers in the advisory roles. Companies tend to capitalize on social learning experiences and analyzing psychosocial dynamics of communities to deliver value to customers. Most customer-centric companies aim at providing desired value and lifestyle (VALS), self-actualization, and comparative self-esteem in the value creation process.

The acquired and shared culture among customers drives awareness about the new trends, which in turn arouses new customer preferences. For example, customer preferences for 3-D games, virtual reality products, and trendy customer electronics influence customers in the emerging markets as "millennial effect." Experience sharing over the digital platforms further influences the customer behavior over a long time. Patterns of consumerism are changing in the society, as there are shifts in the customer demography in the markets. The explosion of mass customer segments, urbanization, and increase in the size of the population of aging customers have contributed significantly to the shifts in customer preferences and overall consumption behavior. Direct-to-customer marketing strategies, convenience shopping, and social media-driven marketing approaches of companies have increased social and cultural influence on developing the customer behavior. However, disruption in technology, and attraction toward local consumption also contribute in driving the customer behavior dynamic across the geo-demographic segments. Extended technology lifecycle builds positive customer perceptions on higher value for money. Co-creation and co-designing approaches of customer-centric companies like IKEA has established business philosophy of connecting customers and developing an emotion-based relationship with customers as the key to leveraging loyalty and advocacy behavior.

Internal factors that influence the perceptual process of customers include propensity of customer learning on the attributes of products, services, and brands in the market and social ambiance. The capability of retaining perceived memories and associated emotions also drives the cognitive process among customers toward validating their brand perceptions. The perception of customers toward shopping is commonly influenced by the social psychodynamics, need, enthusiasm for experimentation, benefit seeking, and obsessive behavioral attributes. Thus, customer perceptions influence customer behavior with their ecosystem, which often creates *me-too* feeling, and induces the pro-perception buying decisions. In addition, perceived benefits in terms of price, associated promotions, and perceived use value of products significantly influence purchase intention. Perceived customers' effectiveness, occupation, and income level also have significant effect on confirming the positive customer perception toward willingness to pay for the product of high-perceived value (Zhao et al. 2018). Commonly, customer-centric companies engaged in creating continuous value and converging design-to-value strategy with the design-to-market strategy involve multiple dilemmas. Focus on customer value might turn expensive to the companies as they have to use resources extensively at the expense of projected profits. Value-based strategies aim for long-term financial performance and firms view such value-based strategic choices risky to gain quick profit leap but appears to be inevitable in the fast-growing competitive market ecosystem. However, value-based strategies are agile and adaptable in following the economies of scale, where scenario-based strategy maps in converging value-based business approaches with the profit goals of the companies (Buytendijk 2010).

An attitude among customers is evolved over the perception, which is an initial phase of customer perception on products and services. It is a stronger dimension of customer perceptions that embeds a set of beliefs toward a brand, company, person, product, service, a marketing or sales event, or a business situation. Attitude can be positive or negative, or can simply appear as a social trend or personal feeling about the product, services, or brands with a strong emotional commitment. Self-perception associated with self-congruence among customers, form attitude among customers toward a specific brand. Customer attitude is developed based on the self-perception and the opinions they publicly express on particular issues encouraging social interactions. Customer attitude is a convergence of perceived expectancy and perceived value evolved through the cognitive process of customer perception (Fishbien and Ajzen 1975). Self-perception is cognitive state of mind, wherein a subject validates his emotions and feelings to perceive the way he deems fits. This is an auto-judgmental cognitive drive that tends to ratify the perceived action by self-laid criteria than following an external standard for validation. Self-perceptions lead to establish self-esteem, self-actualization, and anthropomorphic behavior among the customers. Self-esteem is embedded in the human cognitive system. It is merely a transitory psychological state, which has major contribution to the perceptual and behavioral formation. The self-perception theory suggests that people infer them by looking and validating at their behaviors in case of dilemma of their own attitudes. Self-perception in psychology are widely referred for facial or physical validations as cognitive evidence. Customers often use self-perception or self-reference while stuck with making right choices in shopping products at self-service stores.

The self-perception, propagation of views on the products and services over the social media, celebrity endorsements, and brand promotions support customer attitude, and drive emotional bonding. Such cognitive state of mind stimulates emotions, and customers tend to get associated with the products and services by buying them repeatedly. Most customer-centric companies ensure that customers gain favorable and sustainable perception through brand campaigns, digital communications, social media forums, and product and services trials. In this perceptual mapping process, the cognitive drivers help customers in developing sustainable customer attitude. This situation not only positions the brand as "top-of-mind" element but also encourages repeat buying among the customers. Such an attitude is reflected in the buying behavior and sharing of brand experience extensively over the interpersonal and digital platforms by the customers.

Customers behave in the market in four different ways comprising proactive, reactive, interactive, and inactive. All four ways of expressing customer behavior refer to their cultural background. Proactive customers are experimental to new products, and are prone to accept the cultural changes induced by the market. The proactive customers are largely induced by the markets through lifestyle interventions and cross-cultural fusion. Reactive customers are critical to new products, strategies, and corporate initiatives and prefer the conventional culture that has grown over the period in the society. The reactive customers are aggressive in sharing their experience and are often critical about the products and services of the company. Interactive customers express their views logically and analyze the products and services of a company rationally and comparatively. Inactive customers are passive and nonresponsive. Customers in the acquired culture are prone to behavioral changes, adapt to modern values and are interactive in the market. These attributes of acquired culture drive multinational companies to develop dynamic marketing strategies, build their brand, and augment market share (Rajagopal 2016).

Perceptual Semantics

Semantics exhibits connectivity of thoughts, perceptions, and values among customers on any given object, situation, or within an existing business ecosystem. Cognitive semantics is the continuity of thought process that occurs in human mind. The cognitive semantics emerges as a process of thoughts and communication that connects to a core thought or mental state addressing the specific ecosystem (Brandt 2005). Customers tend to develop compositions of contextual meaning and senses of a given word, phrases, situations, concepts, or acquired information that affects the processing of complex thoughts, perceptions, and emotions. However, research on embodied cognition demonstrates that perceptual semantics is more than just synchronization of thoughts on lexical meanings rather perceptual experience. The semantic thoughts are extensions of a principal thought leading to contextual interpretations and decisions. Therefore, perception-based information such as key terms in communication, advertisements, social media messages, and corporate announcements need to be meticulously drafted and posted. Customers sensitive to the critical appraisals of words and their meaning engage in wooing perceptual semantics to arrive at cognitive synthesis and decisions. Consequently, market communications including word-of-mouth conversations need a transparent and noncomplex array to encourage positive semantic exercise on concepts and embedded meaning of market communication (Günther et al. 2020).

The notion of semantics has been evolved over variations in the use of language, which enables to determine a contextual meaning or its ecosystem. Using cognitive semantics, customers tend to bread contextual meaning of words and perceptions on specific communication keywords. For example, the word "green" might have the semantic expansion to explore the contextual terms such as sustainable, organic, fertilizer, permaculture, natural cultivation, renewal sources, energy, public policy, social consciousness, and the like. Necessarily, the perceptual semantics play as decision drivers in developing awareness, comprehension, conviction, and action (ACCA) paradigm. However, the question of how the meanings of words are represented in the mind is complex as the development of semantics to a specific word or concept is connected with the existing knowledge and past experience of the customers in building semantics. Customers may lean toward positive or negative trail of semantic thoughts based on their repository of knowledge and experience. The earliest views of word meaning in conjunction with the efficiency of cognitive process assumes that words represent as sets of embedded features and theories, which hold magnanimous potential to explain a number of phenomena, contextual comprehension, and build a logical framework of relative concepts, perceptions, and guided decisions. Perceptual semantics also inculcate emotions, impulse, and conscious or unconscious cognitive biasness toward specific context. Consequently, the cognitive semantics-based lexicon ecosystem affects customer values with biased, distorted, or develop negativity in thoughts. Commonly the meaning of words depends not just on how words are defined but on what words, and the phrases and clauses in which they appear, determine the cognitive process (Sanford 2006). Growing concepts in social psychology and neuromarketing experiments endorse that cognitive semantics has been vibrant among the customers today due to updated knowledge and analytical vigor to build appropriate perceptions and buying intentions. The cognitive process, neural network, and social behavior moderate the cognitive semantics process among customers in making buying decisions. One of critical theoretical perspectives of cognitive neuroscience in recent years is the controlled semantic cognition (CSC) framework. This framework proposes that a network of brain areas provides access to sematic information and its appropriate usage. The CSC theory and associated models have been applied to explain wide range of evidence on positive and negative notions of customer neurological effects in decision making by analyzing the available information. The CSC protagonists use the term "semantic cognition" to describe a set of supramodal processes that explain the ecosystems of thoughts woven around the information (keywords and concepts). These processes include the refinement of verbal and nonverbal experiences to form a coherent knowledge base by steering the thoughts within a specific ecosystem of market information (Adolphs 2010).

Semantics is more frequently associated with language skills, which comprehends cognitive thought process and perceptual manifestation and portrays nonverbal behaviors including action perception, object interaction, and a range of socio-cognitive processes. The nonverbal behavior is expressed as empathy, emotions, and communications, which broadly constitutes semantic representational system within hub (desire and need)-and-spoke (perceptual semantics) architecture. This model plays an essential role in acquiring and analyzing information from personal sources and public domain through various social networks, and reviews affective experiences. Broadly, such "embodiment" of connected thoughts is shared among various episodes of semantic memory (Binney and Ramsey 2020). The effects of market dynamics and value foundations on the perceptual semantics are exhibited in Figure 4.2.

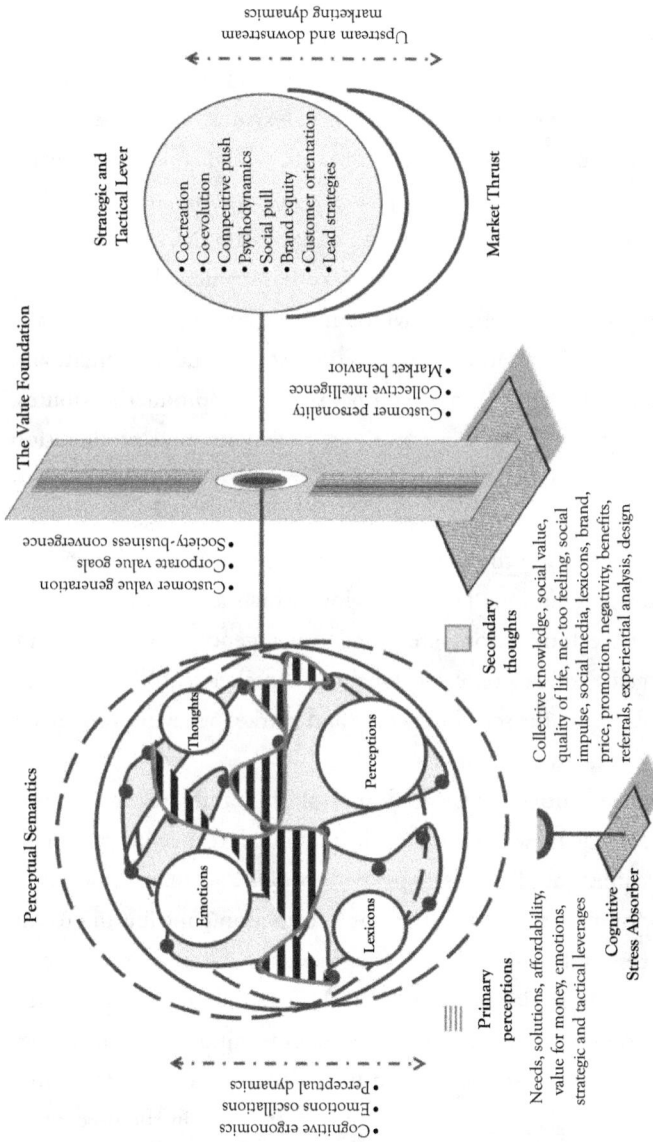

Figure 4.2 Interplay of market dynamics and perceptual semantics on value creation.

Source: Author.

Perceptual semantics, a thought-connecting process in customers, is largely supported by primary perceptions and secondary thoughts as illustrated in Figure 4.2. Primary perceptions are formed by analyzing the individual needs, products, and services solutions to the existing problems, affordability, perceived value for money, and emotions, and the associated short- and long-term benefits. The secondary thoughts based on the collective information, social values, lexicons, and me-too feeling are woven around the primary perceptions, which contribute toward the decision-making process. The primary perceptions and secondary thoughts are driven by the upstream and downstream market thrust. The strategic and tactical market approaches of companies play significant role in driving the market thrust, which include co-creation and coevolution (customer collaboration in innovation, strategy development, and managing communications), and competitive push (product attributes, pricing, delivery of products, promotions, packaging, and proliferation of products within the portfolios). In addition, social pull through community values also contributes to the customer values. The factors driving market thrust moderate the perceptual semantics and cognitive semantics. Accordingly, emotions keep changing, which affects the customer values. The value foundations are based convergence of the corporate value-based goals and customer personality. Nonetheless, collective intelligence, derived from the social networks and market behavior, also affects the customer value in the short term.

Cognitive semantics play significant role in value creation among customers. Managers with large multifunctional teams in customer-centric companies monitor customer perceptions and map variation in their perception to identify the origin of information contributing to the thought process and modify the affecting words, phrases, or information accordingly (Govindarajan and Gupta 2001). The ability to self-generated thoughts in conscious and subconscious state of mind is central to cognition process. Most customers revise their decision many times before buying products or services as they actively participate in the perceptual semantics and spend time in critically examining the available information and shared experiences (Kane et al. 2007). In view of their ubiquity, it is hardly surprising that self-generated thoughts are linked to useful features of human cognition including: planning, temporal decision making, memory, and creative problem solving (Wang et al. 2018). The thought process journey among customers is complex and interrelated to the causes and effects, events, motivations, experiences, and self-learning. The perceptions of customers on any tangible or intangible object or process has vast expansion over the temporal and spatial dimensions, which significantly contribute to building the cognitive ergonomics of customers. Therefore, mind mapping has emerged as a neuromarketing experimental science to understand customer psychology and develop marketing strategies to align with the state of the mind of customers. Mind maps track the natural progression of through process and perceptual semantics by connecting end-to-end thoughts with intermittent moderating thoughts in a linear or discrete path. Each new thought exhibits idea(s) from the ones proceeding and succeeding it, thereby forming the mind map with perceptual semantic thinking process. Mind maps of customers are used in learning customers perceptions on tangible (products) and intangible (services) domains. It is a continuous learning process for the companies to analyze perceptual semantics and customer thought process to develop right customer-centric strategies.

Unconscious thoughts potentially outperform conscious thoughts in making complex choices by products or services in the competitive market. The benefits of unconscious thoughts can be seen when there is an asynchrony between customers' routine preference and the point of purchase decisions. E-commerce customers often face complex product choices and have to make decisions due to complex array of products, which hinders smooth decision making. Viewing at the large assortment of products (e.g., Amazon, Alibaba e-commerce websites) drives multiple perceptions among customers. Most customers undergo the process of mapping perceptual semantics and simultaneously eliminating distracting features to help in deriving conscious decisions. Illusionary and distracting website features further increase the difficulty for customers to make optimal purchase decisions. Choosing a suboptimal product can result in customer regret and product return. Consequently, customers develop decision-making perspectives on both conscious, unconscious, and subconscious thoughts that spur in the mind as perceptual semantics in facilitating complex in brick-and-mortar and online shopping (e.g., Dijksterhuis and Nordgren 2006). Unconscious perceptions about color, size, shape, age, and gender are based on certain natural biases indigenous to an individual's cultural background. Perceptual biases can be divided into two types: cultural and artistic. Cultural biases are naturally occurring environmental observations about the world, while the artistic biases are inherent in the perception of form. These cultural and artistic biases are so entrenched in our subconscious thought that they are unavoidable and automatic. Artistic manipulation of these biases allows the colorful nonverbal contents of a vogue brand to mesmerize the customer's perception and lean decision making toward the brand association and buying the product (Aschheim and Singer 2015).

Behavioral Determinants and Value Perception

Customers exhibit asymmetric buying behavior within multiple cultures and subcultures, which leads to differences in consumption practices. For example, whenever customers adapt to another culture, they may experience cultural shock. Sometimes customers feel that their consumption culture is superior to the acquired culture. The ethnocentrism endorses such customer behavior wherein customers judge the consumption culture of other societies negatively because they have different cultural beliefs. Ethnocentric customers judge other social groups relative to their own ethnic group or culture, especially with concern for language, behavior, customs, and religion. These ethnic distinctions and subdivisions serve to define each ethnicity's unique cultural identity. Customer ethnocentrism is a psychologically driven consumption pattern that refers to customers who believe that products manufactured in their region are superior to those of others. Multinational companies are pursuing emerging markets by introducing new consumption practices and modifying the conventional customer values. Customers in the continuously changing market culture and lifestyles often feel chaotic in streamlining their perceptions toward the brands, companies, and decision leverages. Such cultural dynamics in the global markets also pose recurrent marketing challenges to companies toward developing sustained preferences of customers across proliferation of product categories and brands. The cultural values spread across geo-demographic segments provide the differentiation platform for various customer brands (Kumar et al. 2011). This concept of acquired cultural stimuli describes that customers may develop purchase intentions for a brand in one destination market, but lean toward other destination markets. It is a common belief that signs of customer ethnocentrism by adapting to the acquired culture and consumption pattern does not guarantee permanent change in the social, cultural, and consumption values among customers across geo-demographic segments.

Open business models encourage collective intelligence, collective decisions, and liberal value stream. The business founded on social philosophies like Toms Shoes emphasizes that on every pair of shoes bought from the Toms stores, the company will donate an adequate pair to a child in need. Similarly, Baron Fig,[1] a manufacturer of high-quality notebooks, addresses the needs and expectations of scholars and professional by creating awareness on the impact of paper production using trees and depleting sustainable ecosystem. The company is committed to plant a tree for every notebook sold. Promoting environmental consciousness and responsibility, and overcoming their impact, the Baron Fig is able to generate social value and integrate their business model with design-to-society and design-to-value philosophies. Emerging companies are increasingly adapting to design cube business models along the triadic dimensions of design-to-market, design-to-society, and design-to-value. Such business models are driven by recent socioeconomic developments, sustainable manufacturing, social innovations, and collective intelligence. Besides, vertically integrating the design-thinking based business modeling, the marketing strategies are expanding on horizontal dimension by integrating co-creation, coevolution, and collaborations with large companies. Incorporating these dimensions, the business model archetypes can holistically capture the increasing openness in developing strategies and engaging customers in the emerging closed-loop value chain (Kortmann and Piller 2016).

Contrary to ethnocentrism, customer following xenocentrism,[2] easily adapt to external consumption culture as they believe that the external

---

[1] For details see https://baronfig.com/

[2] Xenocentrism in social psychology is defined as the preference of people for the products, styles, or ideas of external culture, which may be of a country, region, society, or an individual over their own.

consumption culture is better than the existing one. The increasing market competition, experience marketing, sharing information on social media, and customer research have turned the customers xenocentric. Such consumption philosophy has developed cross-cultural consumption behavior among the customers in the developed and emerging markets. The metropolitan and urban customer culture is largely xenocentric and is more powerful in driving the marketing strategies of most companies. Culture influences many aspects of marketing mix in the host country. An international firm makes its market-oriented decisions in reference to the various customer perspectives that are determined by customer lifestyles and behavior patterns. The cultural aspects largely affect the products that people buy, the attributes that value, and the referrals that govern the buying decisions of the customers. Culture creates the system of communication among customer about acceptance and rejection of the products and services, for example, food. Influence of Italian cultural in global markets plays an important role for the creation or expansion of markets for Italian products (Rajagopal and Castaño 2015). Customers experience brands emotionally, not through individual communications, that is, advertising, packaging, online presence, or promotions, but in their totality. There exists in every country a *culture screen*, which generates cognitive and affective influences, and shapes the interpersonal and personal determinants to form the customer behavior.

The general culture defines a set of acceptable and unacceptable behaviors within the social norms. Individuals should learn to act according to these behavioral norms, while managers need to learn how to do business. These are the processes of enculturation and socialization. They determine how individuals behave as customers in the marketplace, how demanding they are, how they voice complaints, how managers approach subordinates and peers, and so forth. In due course of time, individuals become skilled in exhibiting acceptable behaviors and identifying the unacceptable behaviors in order to be less risk averse. An American marketer is good at briefly presenting his or her point of view, while the Japanese counterpart is good at listening. However, going beyond one's accustomed norms is hard to do. It is difficult to map customer perceptions and measure value propositions accurately as it is psychologically complicated. However, general conventions about understanding the customer value do exist by way of creating innovative experience, value for money, and satisfaction in tune to the self-congruence. These measures toward customer value pay off in terms of stronger customer loyalty, greater customer willingness to try a particular brand, and sustained revenue growth. The deeper analysis of "elements of value" has its conceptual roots to Maslow's "hierarchy of needs" and extends focusing on customers toward understanding their behavior around products and services. The core elements of value can be arrayed in a pyramid with reference to "functional values" at the bottom, followed by emotional, quality of life, and social values at the peak. Most customer products companies have invested resources in improving these elements to grow revenue, refine product design to better meet customers' needs, identify customers' core perceived strengths and weaknesses, and cross-sell brands (Almquist et al. 2016).

Customer behavior is largely catalyzed by collective influence as customers tend to match their personal attributes with the social and cultural values. The customer behavior is manifested in crowd psycho-dynamics and collective value perspectives, by constructing the individual value (i.e., sense of self) and developing self-image congruence with the crowd behavior. Collective knowledge tends to maximize customers value by learning and sharing experiences and rebuild social value perspectives. Accordingly, customers construct their identities through pooled knowledge, perceptual semantics, and rebuilding self-identity (Fedorenko et al. 2017). Customers develop insights from peer conversations on digital networks about products and services. Such social knowledge helps in identifying hybrid notions on value chain management, and linking customer perceptions and expectations with the market attributes in general, and corporate goals in particular. On digital networks, customer knowledge is leveraged as a community to create value not only for the customers but also for the social involved firms. It is a customer-determined value nurtured by the firms by developing appropriate social and business ecosystems to drive bidirectional engagement social and sustainable development besides offering competitive leverage to customers (Belk 2013).

Customers develop sustainable perceived use values if the product attractiveness is endorsed by the brand awareness and brand experience. In addition to newness of the products, vogue, social value, ethnic perceptions, and customer beliefs inculcate the experiential attitude among customers. Most customer-centric companies develop new products as "design-to-value" by involving customers in co-creation process. Such customer engagements in new product development help companies manage seasonality of products effectively in the marketplace, and develop sustainable customer attitude and consumption behavior. Therefore, it observed that like product seasonality, customer behavior also turns seasonal over time. The customer value chain often supports seasonality of customer behavior (Rajagopal 2019). Customer value in terms of satisfaction, use value, retailing practices, price, quality, and media appreciation is one of the indicators for building brand value for the nonconventional products and unfamiliar brands of a firm. Firms evaluate the product performance of an innovative product in the given market and determine the approach for gaining competitive advantage over the traditional products may apply customer value concepts. In order to gain returns on the aggregate customer value in the long term, firms need to estimate the profitability associated thereof in terms of product attractiveness, volume of buying, and market share while introducing the new products in a competitive market environment.

Customer Lifetime Value

Customer value is dynamic, and it shifts with the growth of innovation, technology, market leverage, and peer experience. Social media networks contribute in creating awareness and sharing community views on the competitive products and services. The focus on value perspectives among customers dynamically shifts from resources and benefits of products and services to orchestrating them to gain lifetime value. However, firms are able to generate customer values by facilitating more external interactions and creating network effects to develop consistent feeling among customers and build lifetime value. In the contemporary market situation, the customer value is largely affected by market competition that provide ad hoc benefits to the customers and stakeholder to manage the lead. Most companies are able to determine the customer loyalty alongside the objective of achieving *performance with purpose* by optimizing the activities in their value chains, which they own or control. Socially conscious companies, such as Uber, Alibaba, and Airbnb, intervene in social media channels (public) and customer experience channels (owned and controlled) to bring customers together with corporate business policies (Van Alstyne et al. 2016). Such customer engagement in co-creating values has emerged as a strong social differentiator to create lifetime value, loyalty, and lead in business (3-L factors). However, successfully managing the customer engagement requires a social approach (design-to-society) to build value-driven strategy. Effective customer engagement has therefore emerged as a necessary tool to manage business transition from the conventional approaches of business (market driven profit) to achieve performance with purpose (value-driven profit).

Customer lifetime value (CLV) is a key metric within customer relationship management. Although a large number of marketing scientists and practitioners argue in favor of this metric, there are only a few studies that consider the predictive modeling of CLV. In these industries, customer behavior is rather complex, because customers can purchase more than one service, and these purchases are often not independent from each other (Donkers et al. 2003). However, it has been observed that low perceived use value, comparative advantages over physical attributes, and economic gains of the product make a significant impact on determining the customer value for relatively new products. The customer value gap may be defined as the negative driver that lowers the returns on the aggregate customer value. This is an important variable, which needs to be carefully examined by a firm, and its impact on the profitability of the firm needs to be measured in reference to spatial (coverage of the market) and temporal (over time) market dimension.

Customer engagement in businesses significantly contributes to the success of companies in the competitive marketplace. Value creation is a bidirectional process from a company to customers and vice versa. Customers help in generating value to a company through outside-in push to build the brands and loyalty, while the companies drive inside-out pull to accommodate customers with their perceptual and emotional values, competitive gains, and toward developing brand trust. In building customer values, companies stay transparent in their business goals, marketing and for-profit strategies, and social orientation profit. Customers share their views on the value generation process and react to them on social media, which helps companies proceed with the co-created value generation policies upon possible incorporation of the views of customers and stakeholders. Accordingly, firms plan toward acquiring value perspectives and acknowledging, leveraging, and disseminating values. The value co-created through the previous process emerges as a strategic marketing tool for creating customer value (Mills 2015).

One of the principal drivers of customer behavior is the dominance of social interactions. The involvement of customers in co-creation depends not only on their own perceptions but also on the peers' response to their personality and change proneness (Pinheiro 2008). The relation between clothes and identity is perceived by customers from the perspective of their values generated in various social interactions. Customers get involved in exhibiting lifestyle as an aesthetic way of presenting their personality. Hence, clothing is often considered as an opportunity to communicate a new order of identity of a person. In this process, there are both cognitive and affective incentives that translate into potential welfare gains (or indifference) for the customer in a given social and work-related environment (Bianchi 2002). Contemporary researchers have emphasized that a firm must manage customer relationships for the long term for maximizing the lifetime value of customers. In disagreement to this notion, a study demonstrates that profits in competitive environments are maximized when managers focus on the short term with respect to their customers (Villanueva et al. 2004). The competitive implications of a switch to a long-term customer focus must be carefully examined before such a switch is advocated or implemented. Paradoxically, customer lifetime value is maximized when managers focus on the short-term benefits for customers.

Customers today are extensively influenced by the experience of society in general and peers in particular. Therefore, values are often derived collaboratively on the digital networks, and marketing is evolving on the social conversations and collective intelligence. Customer-centric companies are practicing controlled marketing communications by filtering the social media communication and responding to customer questions through corporate spokespeople, which help in managing the messy social messages. Amidst the growth of parallel social channels, the user-generated content predominantly moderates the customer values and the strategy development process at the corporate level (Muñiz and Schau 2011). The role of customer value has been largely recognized by the firms as an instrument toward stimulating market share and profit optimization. The customer values for a new product in the competitive markets are shaped more by habits, reinforcement effects, and situational influences than strongly held attitudes. The customer value is an intangible factor, which plays a significant role in influencing the buying decisions. The customer value broadly includes psychometric variables like brand name, loyalty, satisfaction, and referral opinions. The customer lifetime value is built over time by the business firms, which also contributes to the individual perceptions of the customers and augments their value.

In the growing competitive markets, large and reputed firms are developing strategies to move into the provision of innovative combinations of products and services as "high-value integrated solutions" tailored to each customer's needs than simply "moving downstream" into services. Such firms are developing innovative combinations of service capabilities such as operations, business consultancy, and finance required to provide complete solutions to each customer's needs in order to augment the customer value toward the innovative or new products. It has been argued that the provision of integrated solutions is attracting the firms traditionally based in manufacturing and services to occupy a new base in the value stream centered on "systems integration" using internal or external sources of product designing, supply, and customer focused promotion (Davies 2004). Besides the organizational perspectives of enhancing the customer value, the functional variables like pricing play a significant role in developing the customer perceptions toward the new products. The key marketing variables such as price, brand name, and product attributes affect customers' judgment process, and derive inference on its quality dimensions leading to customer satisfaction. An experimental study conducted indicates that customers use price and brand name differently to judge the quality dimensions and measure the degree of satisfaction (Brucks et al. 2000). The value of corporate brand endorsement across different products and product lines, and at lower levels of the brand hierarchy, also needs to be assessed as a customer value driver. Use of corporate brand endorsement, either as a name identifier or as logo, identifies the product with the company, and provides reassurance for the customer (Rajagopal and Sanchez 2004).

Analysis of the perceived values of customers toward new products is a complex issue. Despite considerable research in the field of measuring customer values in the recent past, it is still not clear how value interacts with marketing-related constructs. However, a comprehensive application model determining the interrelationship between customer satisfaction and customer value is needed, which may help in reducing the ambiguities surrounding both concepts. Systematic analysis of customer value in the previous studies indicates convergence of the following values:

- Perceived values
- Cultural values
- Personal values
- Consumption values
- Aesthetic and hedonic values
- Social and family values
- Purchase convenience and postpurchase values, and
- Monetary values

Improving customer value through faster response times for new products is a significant way to gain competitive advantage. In the globalization process, many approaches to new product development emerge, which exhibit an internal focus, and view the new product development process as terminating with product launch.

Managing market competition and simultaneously creating customer value is a complex task for companies. Prioritizing value generation while securing the competitive position is often conflictive for the companies as most companies focus on implementing the competitive marketing strategies and stay tactical. Customer value generation is a strategic process, and, while companies are in competition, they intend to generate as much value as possible from every transaction. Consequently, firms use pricing as tool to create customer value, and customers often fight the unfair pricing policies of the firms. Most companies think of customer value as a pie of gross revenue. Therefore, the value is not proportionately fixed, which disappoints customers and they reject the pricing linked value-creation strategies. Alternatively, companies can use it to enlarge the pie in lieu of implementing pricing-based value strategies considering customers as business associates in value creation. The pricing-based value creation can be enhanced by the firms through customer engagement and the following associated measures by:

- Focusing on long-term, value-based customer relationships than developing transactional relationship
- Using pricing strategy as a communication tool to create customer values by developing value for money and perceived satisfaction
- Setting proactive prices to discourage detrimental behavior and to encourage mutual benefits to both customers and firms
- Setting prices ethically by justifying the corporate response to shifting customer needs
- Promoting transparency by providing the corporate rationale in pricing, and
- Assuring prices and processes of pricing strategy to meet customers' expectations

A collaborative customer-value-creation strategy increases customer engagement, though which firms can explore customer expectations, value delivery options, and insights about the value they seek and how firms could deliver it. Such value generation strategies not only augment the revenue bowl of the firm but also help in enhancing customer satisfaction, loyalty, and positive word-of-mouth and experience sharing on social media (Bertini and Gourville 2012).

Companies today create customer value by driving customers toward destination brands, which embed cross-cultural emotions and ethnicity. Some companies like Apple, Samsung, and Cadbury's are routinely testing innovations with rich customer-transaction data within cultural and ethnic diversities. Introduced a random change in customer culture has become a radical approach to inculcate new values among customers. The digital space like websites, commercial blogs, and social media platforms including Facebook are being extensively used to mitigate customer anomalies in adapting to new customer culture and adapting modern values of consumption. Most companies that adopt a *test and learn* culture to promote new trends tend to realize the greatest benefits by stimulating customers to stay along vogue, and gain enhanced customer values. Commonly, tactical decisions such as choosing a new store format and recreational retaining strategies of companies attract customers and set in the new value trends (Davenport 2009).

Customer satisfaction includes location convenience, one-stop shopping convenience, and reputation of the company besides the corporate policies on acquiring and retaining customers. Trust and satisfaction play different mediating roles in the relationships between service attributes, customer retention, and cross buying (Liu and Wu 2007). Relationship value is an antecedent to relationship quality and behavioral outcomes, and displays a stronger impact on satisfaction than on commitment and trust. Value also directly affects a customer's intention to expand business with a supplier. In turn, its impact on the propensity to leave a relationship is mediated by relationship quality (Voss et al. 2005). The value of relationship with the customer reveals significant quality and behavioral outcomes in the sales activities. Value displays a stronger impact on satisfaction than on commitment and trust and directly affects a customer's intention to expand business with the firm. The perceived strength of the relationship with the customers may be measured by the salespeople in reference to technical ability, experience, pricing requirements, speed of response, frequency of customer contact, degree of cooperation, trust, length of relationship, friendship, and management distance barriers (Rajagopal 2009).

Customers have experienced the changing values with the shifts in business trends such as deregulation, globalization, frugal innovations, global-local technological convergence, and the rapid evolution of e-commerce. Such changes in the business systems have transformed the strategies of creating customer value through social alliances, networks, and customer collaboration with companies. Co-created innovation and technology-led products enable firms to engage customers in active dialogue with community though social media channels as a major tool in creating value. The customer engagement in co-creating the values includes engagement in active social-business dialogues, sharing thoughts, and business ideas explicitly, mobilizing digital and neighborhood customer, managing beliefs and trust, and sociocultural diversities. Companies, therefore, periodically revise traditional value creation strategies of customers (Prahalad and Ramaswamy 2000).

The modern market has emerged with the announcement that ethnic dressing comes from the core of the traditional culture, whose gorgeous fabrics have been facelifted as convenience apparel within societal value and lifestyle (VALS) system. It is argued that shifts in customer culture provide a stimulus to dynamic innovation in the arena of personal taste and consumption. Such dynamism in customer preferences is considered as part of an international cultural system and is driven by a continuous change in VALS. The customer values like functionality, fitness for purpose, and efficiency significantly contribute in driving cultural change and recognizing suitable lifestyles (Hartley and Montgomery 2009). The growing technology-led apparel selling is one of the major stimulants for inducing change in fashion and customer culture. The three-dimensional Automatic Made-to-Measure scheme for apparel products demonstrated through computer simulation in large departmental stores and lifestyle centers plays a major role in creating cognitive arousal among customers. To represent the complex geometry models of apparel products, the apparel designers, manufacturers, and retailers adopt freeform design platform. Apparel products are essentially designed with reference to human body features and share a common set of features as the human model. Therefore, the parametric, feature-based modeling enables the automatic generation of fitted garments on differing body shapes. Customers lean toward buying such apparel that are largely sold as designer apparel (Wang et al. 2005).

Summary

Customer behavior can be explained with the attributes of social cognitive theory, which argues that self-regulation and self-efficacy guide the buying behavior and develop social-personal congruence in cognitive thought process. Behavioral attributes influence customer perceptions toward the contextual, sociocultural and personal relevance of a product or service, which contribute to the lifestyle, values, and satisfaction. Social learning process is widely influenced by the manifold growth of social media, digital networks, and interpersonal communications. Information technology has dramatically changed the social communication inflow with customers sharing their experiences, values, new product ideas, and complaints about companies during their shopping experiences. Customer behavior in the competitive marketplace is widely influenced by discretionary spending, buying low-cost products, and seeking value for money. Companies practicing incremental marketing technologies are able to understand the dynamics of customer preferences by using digital data analytics, social media-driven consumption patterns, and customer experience through virtual reality.

The value perceptions among customers with utilitarian perspectives reflect rational, instrumental, and task-related consumption, while the hedonic dimensions correspond to affective, emotional, and luxury values and lifestyle. This value-driven marketing strategy is compatible with the design cube concept, wherein companies converge design-to-market strategies with design-to-society and design-to-value strategies. Customers are also often interested in higher satisfaction by consuming innovative and socially differentiated products to achieve self-realization, fairness, freedom, participation, social relations, and balance among the consumption ecosystem. Customer perceptions are often agile and need to be endorsed by the peers, friends, and family to support decision making and to put them into practice over the long term. Customers generally measure their perceived values in reference to the desired satisfaction in terms of value for money derived through the convergence of quality and price.

Co-created customer values help companies focus customer-centric product offerings to gain competitive leverage. Upon understanding the perceptions, emotions, values of customers, companies make smarter choices about allocating resources in customer services, advertisement and communications, and implementing marketing-mix-driven strategies. The co-created and coevolved customer value constructs are able to deliver optimal benefits to customers by upholding their perceptions, choices, and self-esteem. Large companies with strategic focus on customers develop value dashboard to monitor customer touchpoints, which helps in co-creating customer value proposition. Social and cultural values influence customers' personal values and alter cognitive dynamics comprising attention, semantics, memory, perception, problem-solving abilities, creativity, conscious thinking, and decision rationale. The cognitive value assessment is a major task in understanding the underlying personal, social, and cultural values among customers in the conscious and subconscious states of mind.

The value creation is broadly a derivation of conscious cognition, actions in subconscious mind, unconscious perceptions, and materialistic reasoning. The cognitive ergonomics of customers (emotions, perceptions, and memories and storyboards), knowledge, beliefs, trust, and the ability of information analysis constitute the conscious cognition, which embeds customer value perceptions. In the corporate context, the design-to-value perspectives include co-creation of customer value and coevolving business by engaging customers in the advisory roles. Companies tend to capitalize on social learning experiences and analyzing psychosocial dynamics of communities to deliver value to customers. Commonly, customer-centric companies engaged in creating continuous value, and converging design-to-value strategy with the design-to-market strategy, involve multiple dilemmas. Focus on customer value might turn expensive to the companies as they have to use resources extensively at the expense of projected profits.

Cognitive semantics is the continuity of thought process that occurs in human mind. Customers tend to develop compositions of contextual meaning and senses of given words, phrases, situations, concepts, or acquired information that affect the processing of complex thoughts, perceptions, and emotions. Using cognitive semantics, customers tend to breed contextual meaning of words and perceptions on specific communication keywords. The cognitive process, neural network, and social behavior moderate the cognitive semantics process among customers in making buying decisions. Cognitive semantics play significant role in value creation among customers. Most customers revise their decision many times before buying products or services as they actively participate in the perceptual semantics and spend time in critically examining the available information and shared experiences. The thought process journey among customers is complex and interrelated to the causes and effects, events, motivations, experiences, and self-learning. Customers exhibit asymmetric buying behavior within multiple cultures and subcultures, which leads to differences in consumption practices. The thought process journey among customers is complex and interrelated to the causes and effects, events, motivations, experiences, and self-learning. Mind maps track the natural progression of through process and perceptual semantics by connecting end-to-end thoughts with intermittent moderating thoughts in a linear or discrete path.

Customer value is dynamic and it shifts with the growth of innovation, technology, market leverage, and peer experience. Social media networks contribute in creating awareness and sharing community views on the competitive products and services. The focus on value perspectives among customers dynamically shifts from resources and benefits of products and services to orchestrating them to gain lifetime value. Most companies are able to determine the customer loyalty alongside the objective of achieving *performance with purpose* by optimizing the activities in their value chains, which they own or control. Customer engagement in businesses significantly contributes to the success of companies in competitive marketplace. Value creation is a bidirectional process from a company to customers and vice versa. Customers today are extensively influenced by the experience of peers in particular and society in general. Therefore, values are often derived collaboratively on the digital networks, and marketing is evolving on the social conversations and collective intelligence. Customer value generation is a strategic process, and, while companies are in competition, they intend to generate as much value as possible from every transaction. A collaborative customer value creation strategy increases customers' engagement though which firms can explore customer insights, expectations, and value delivery options. insights about the value they seek and how firms could deliver it.

References

Adolphs, R. 2010. "Conceptual Challenges and Directions for Social Neuroscience." *Neuron* 65, pp. 752–776.

Almquist, E., J. Senior, and N. Bloch. 2016. "The Elements of Value." *Harvard Business Review* 94, no. 9, pp. 47–53.

Anderson, J.C., and J.A. Narus. 1999. "Business Marketing; Understand What Customers Value." *Harvard Business Review* 76, no. 6, pp. 53–65.

Anderson, J.C., J.A. Narus, and W. Van Rossum. 2006. "Customer Value Propositions in Business Markets." *Harvard Business Review* 84, no. 3, pp. 91–99.

Aschheim, K.W., and B.A. Singer. 2015. "Fundamentals of Esthetics and Smile Analysis." In *Esthetic Dentistry* ed. K.W. Aschheim, 38–54, 3rd ed. Maryland Heights: Mosby Publishing.

Belk, R. 2013. "Extended Self in a Digital World." *Journal of Customer Research* 40, no. 3, pp. 477–500.

Bertini, M., and J.T. Gourville. 2012. "Pricing to Create Shared Value." *Harvard Business Review* 90, no. 6, pp. 96–104.

Bianchi, M. 2002. "Novelty, Preferences, and Fashion: When Goods are Unsettling." *Journal of Economic Behavior & Organization* 47, no. 1, pp. 1–18.

Binney, R.J., and R. Ramsey. 2020. "Social Semantics: The Role of Conceptual Knowledge and Cognitive Control in a Neurobiological Model of the Social Brain." *Neuroscience & Biobehavioral Reviews* 112, no. 1, pp. 28–38.

Brandt, P.A. 2005. "Mental Spaces and Cognitive Semantics: A Critical Comment." *Journal of Pragmatics* 37, no. 10, pp. 1578–1594.

Brucks, M., V.A. Zeithaml, and G. Naylor. 2000. "Price and Brand Name as Indicators of Quality Dimensions of Customer Durables." *Journal of Academy of Marketing Science* 28, no. 3, pp. 359–374.

Buytendijk, F. 2010. *Dealing with Dilemmas: Redefining Strategy*. Harvard Business School Publishing Newsletter, Cambridge: Harvard Business School.

Davenport, T.H. 2009. "How to Design Smart Business Experiments." *Harvard Business Review* 87, no. 2, pp. 68–77.

Davies, A. 2004. "Moving Base into High-value Integrated Solutions: A Value Stream Approach." *Industrial and Corporate Change* 13, no. 5, pp. 727–756.

Dijksterhuis, A., and L.F. Nordgren. 2006. "A Theory of Unconscious Thought." *Perspectives on Psychological Science* 1, no. 2, pp. 95–109.

Donkers, B., P.C. Verhoef, and D.J. Martijn. April, 2003. *Predicting Customer Lifetime Value in Multi-service Industries*, ERIM Report Series.

Fedorenko, I., P. Berthon, and T. Rabinovich. 2017. "Crowded Identity: Managing Crowdsourcing Initiatives to Maximize Value for Participants through Identity Creation." *Business Horizons* 60, no. 2, pp. 155–165.

Fishbien, M., and I. Ajzen. 1975. *Belief, Attitude, Intention, and Behavior: An Introduction to Theory and Research*. Reading, MA, Addison-Wesley.

Govindarajan, V., and A.K. Gupta. 2001. "Building an Effective Global Business Team." *MIT Sloan Management Review* 42, no. 4, pp. 63–71.

Günther, F., M.A. Petilli, and M. Marelli. 2020. "Semantic Transparency is not Invisibility: A Computational Model of Perceptually-Grounded Conceptual Combination in Word Processing." *Journal of Memory and Language* 112, pp. 1–16.

Hartley, J., and L. Montgomery. 2009. "Fashion as Customer Entrepreneurship: Emergent Risk Culture, Social Network Markets, and the Launch of *Vogue* in China." *Chinese Journal of Communication* 2, no. 1, pp. 61–76.

Jones, M.A., K.E. Reynolds, and M.J. Arnold. 2006. "Hedonic and Utilitarian Shopping Value: Investigating Differential Effects on Retail Outcomes." *Journal of Business Research* 59, no. 9, pp. 974–981.

Kane, M.J., A.R.A. Conway, T.K. Miura, and G.J.H. Colflesh. 2007. "Working Memory, Attention Control, and the N-Back Tasks." *Journal of Experimental Psychology: Learning, Memory, and Cognition* 33, no. 5, pp. 615–622.

Kortmann, S., and F.T. Piller. 2016. "Open Business Models and Closed-Loop Value Chains: Redefining the Firm-Customer Relationship." *California Management Review* 58, no. 3, pp. 88–108.

Kumar, S.R., N. Guruvayurappan, and M. Banerjee. 2011. *Ethnic Customers Consulting*. Cambridge, MA: Harvard Business School Press.

Liu, T.C., and L.W. Wu. 2007. "Customer Retention and Cross-Buying in the Banking Industry: An Integration of Service Attributes, Satisfaction and Trust." *Journal of Financial Services Marketing* 12, no. 2, pp. 132–145.

Martin-Herran, G., S. P. Sigue, and G. Zaccour. 2010. "The Dilemma of Pull and Push-Price Promotions." *Journal of Retailing* 86, no. 1, pp. 51–68.

Mills, A.J. 2015. "Everyone Loves a Secret: Why Customers Value Marketing Secrets." *Business Horizons* 58, no. 6, pp. 643–649.

Muñiz, A.M., and Schau. 2011. "How to Inspire Value-Laden Collaborative Customer-Generated Content." *Business Horizons* 54, no. 3, pp. 209–217.

Pfeffer, J., T. Zorbach, and K.M. Carley. 2014. "Understanding Online Firestorms: Negative Word-of-Mouth Dynamics in Social Media Networks." *Journal of Market Communication* 20, nos. (1–2), pp. 117–128.

Pinheiro, M. 2008. "Loyalty, Peer Group Effects, and 401(k)." *The Quarterly Review of Economics and Finance* 48, no. 1, pp. 94–122.

Prahalad, C.K., and V. Ramaswamy. 2000. "Co-opting Customer Competence." *Harvard Business Review* 78, no. 1, pp. 79–87.

Rajagopal, and R. Sanchez. 2004. "Conceptual Analysis of Brand Architecture and Relationships within Product Category". *Journal of Brand Management* 11, no. 3, pp. 233–247.

Rajagopal and R. Castano. 2015. *Understanding Customer Behaviour and Consumption Experience*. Hershey, PA: IGI Global.

Rajagopal. 2016. *Sustainable Growth in Global Markets: Strategic Choices and Managerial Implications*. Basingstoke, UK: Palgrave Macmillan.

Rajagopal. 2019. *Contemporary Marketing Strategy: Analyzing Customer Behavior to Drive Managerial Decision Making*. New York, NY: Palgrave Macmillan.

Reichheld, F., and W. Earl Sasser Jr. 1990. "Zero Defections: Quality Comes to Services." *Harvard Business Review* 68, no. 5, pp. 105–111.

Sanford, A.J. 2006. "Semantics in Psychology." In *Encyclopedia of Language & Linguistics* ed. K. Brown, 152–158, 2nd ed. Amsterdam: Elsevier.

Sharpe, K.M., and R. Staelin. 2010. "Consumption Effects of Bundling: Consumer Perceptions, Firm Actions, and Public Policy Implications." *Journal of Public Policy & Marketing* 29, no. 2, pp. 170–188.

Treadgold, A., and J. Reynolds. 2016. *Navigating the new retail landscape: A guide for business leaders*. Oxford, UK: Oxford University Press.

Van Alstyne, M.W., G. Parker, and S.P. Choudary. 2016. "Pipelines, Platforms, and the New Rules of Strategy." *Harvard Business Review* 94, no. 4, pp. 54–62.

Verhoef, P.C., P.K. Kannan, and J.J. Inman. 2015. "From Multi-Channel Retailing to Omni-Channel Retailing: Introduction to the Special Issue on Multi-Channel Retailing." *Journal of Retailing* 91, no. 2, pp. 174–181.

Villanueva, J. 2013. "Reading the Signs of Your Customer Value." *IESE-Insight Magazine* 17, no. 2, pp. 24–29.

Villanueva, J., P. Bharadwaj, Y. Chen, and S. Balasubramanian. 2004. *Managing Customer Relationships-Should Managers Really Focus on Long Term*. IESE Business School, Working Paper # D/560, May, pp. 1–37.

Venkatesh, A., A. Joy, J.F. Sherry, and J. Deschenes. 2010. "The Aesthetics of Luxury Fashion, Body and Identify Formation." *Journal of Consumer Psychology* 20, no. 4, pp. 459–470.

Voss, M.D., R.J. Calantone, and S.B. Keller. 2005. "Internal Service Quality: Determinants of Distribution Center Performance." *International Journal of Physical Distribution & Logistics Management* 35, no. 3, pp. 161–176.

Wakefield, K.L., and J.J. Inman. 2003. "Situational Price Sensitivity: The Role of Consumption Occasion, Social Context and Income." *Journal of Retailing* 79, no. 4, pp. 199–212.

Wang, C.C.L., Y. Wang, and M.M.F. Yuen. 2005. "Design Automation for Customized Apparel Products." *Computer-Aided Design* 37, no. 7, pp. 675–691.

Wang, H.T., G. Poerio, C. Murphy, D. Bzdok, E. Jefferies, and J. Smallwood. 2018. "Dimensions of Experience: Exploring the Heterogeneity of the Wandering Mind." *Psychological Science* 29, no. 1, pp. 56–71.

Zhao, R., Y. Geng, Y. Liu, X. Tao, and B. Xue. 2018. "Customers' Perception, Purchase Intention, and Willingness to Pay for Carbon-Labeled Products: A Case Study of Chengdu in China." *Journal of Cleaner Production* 171, no. 1, pp. 1664–1671.

CHAPTER 5

The Helix Effect

Overview

Innovation, social engagement, and co-creation of customer-centric value is an integrated part of the modern business process. The business modeling today is motivated more by the social and customer value-related attributes than by the market competition. This chapter discusses business modeling process in the context of value-driven indicators. The double and triple helix effects on business modeling have been discussed in the chapter in the context of growing design market, design-to-society, and design-to-value philosophies. This chapter deliberates upon the changing issues concerning market competition and value creation strategies. In addition, three cases studies on Apple Inc., IKEA, and Hindustan Unilever Limited (India), which are congruent with the business design-cube canvas, have also been discussed in this chapter.

Innovation has shifted from technology to business models and is more focused on marketing than the social needs. Many innovations are emerging in the market that involve simplifying or improving the existing products or services, and positioning them as innovations. However, managers may align their business strategies with competitive advantages of markets and manage innovation in emerging economies to diffuse and commercialize (De Meyer 2011). The theoretical framework of helix effect explains collaboration and synchronization with different factors on business modeling and innovation. The customer engagement to co-create innovations increases the scope of performance of firms in social and customer-centric innovations. The synchronization of the process of frugal and reverse innovation (corporate alliances for commercialization of local innovations) with business modeling constitute the double helix effect, while these factors, combined with government (public policies), drive the triple helix effect. Broadly, the industry, stakeholders including customers, and the government serve as the agents of triple helix. Some studies confirm that the higher the number of helices involved in innovation, the greater the likelihood of business innovation. Over time, society has also emerged as a community agent to form the quadruple helix, which attracts both government and industry to collaborate in the innovation process (Un and Asakawa 2015). Positioning innovation of products and services makes a company competitive, as believed traditionally, is a myth in the present state of global marketing. Consequently, firms continually reinvent in large and small ways in reference to shifts in market demand and changes in the economy and develop competitive marketing strategy in reference to the shifts in the product and market behavior, knowledge of innovative products, and innovation positions. Though the firms may develop efficiency with regard to the aforementioned strategic positions of product/market, knowledge, and innovation independently, they are still risk-averse with the innovation (McDonough et al. 2008).

Business Modeling

Customer-centric and value-based business models have been a topic of debate since the inception of globalization in the mid-20th century. Business modeling is practiced conventionally, but growing technology has driven multiagent modeling involving coopetition (cooperative competition), society, customers, stakeholders, collective intelligence, and public policies. Successful business models combine business strategies with social competence and technology-based applications to enhance market performance and customer outreach. However, developing business models with multiple agents is complex as they are susceptible to unwarranted risk factor (changes in sociopolitical philosophy, public policies, corporate strategies, and the trend of market competition). Consequently, firms put the multiagent business model into the risk of investing time and resources in implementation. An effective business modeling process entails not only the synergy among the business agents but also the organization culture to implement the business model within various types of markets. Business models can be made easy by developing as a storyboard for customers and stakeholders to understand. The complex business model contains the resource-based inputs, performance dashboard, social value matrix, and future proliferations. The social value-based business models need to define customers and their innate perceptions my mapping them on the storyboard and explain the underlying expectation of social and economic value rationale. Business models describe the system of interconnected business philosophies, which motivates firms to develop appropriate strategies considering the market competition as a critical dimension (Magretta 2002).

Firms also engage the innovation facilities group to explore new developments in the marketplace on the concept, prototypes, or breakthrough of the innovation, and impart expert services for in-house initiatives to nurture innovation within the organization. The innovation assimilation group acts as policy support unit to drive innovation to market. The members of this team provide resources to launch innovation and integrate operations into the business model of the firm. Firms need the aforementioned support teams to diffuse innovation and make it more (Cash et al. 2008). A successful customer-centric project can be developed by the companies by empowering consumers, educating consumers on market competition, and attributes of competitors to enable the right decision making, getting customers to choose a particular business over its competitors, enunciating new market segments, and delivering an integrated experience on buying and consumption. Empowering stakeholders in customer-centric projects is a psychosocial construct related to the individual's perception within the societal framework. Increasing competition in the global markets has pushed companies to stay customer-centric and consider improving the convenience to the customers as prime decision-making parameter. There appears a big dilemma among many companies whether to make a seamless transition to the change or to cordon their markets with the existing products and plunge into niche until they could develop the new business model to cope with the technology change and new manufacturing process. However, at times, both strategies may not sustain to compete with the change in the marketplace (Rajagopal 2016).

The increasing market competition in local and global business spaces is focused on business model innovation as an alternative or a complement to product or process innovation, and on staying competitive in the market. Broadly, a business model is considered as an interconnected and interdependent log of activities that determines the way the company portrays its role in the market along with customers and key partners.

Successful business models embed perceived needs of the market and the key partners associated with the firm by incorporating customized activities (services and values), forward or backward integration, and building the co-creation and coevolution approaches. Frequent changes to business model design may disrupt not only cause lowering the performance of a firm but also affect the functionality of an industry in long term. For effective implementation of business models, firms must consider understanding the perceived needs of customers, stakeholders, and key operations partners; encouraging co-created activities to meet the perceived needs; enhancing the outreach through the social media to build collective intelligence; developing accountability in delivering tasks; co-creating values; and designing the best fit to the market system and growth prospects (Amit and Zott 2012).

Most firms believe that competing through business models is critical for success; but developing appropriate business strategies to push technology and innovations through the business models is a difficult task. Technology firms focus on creating innovative models and evaluating their efficacy. However, the success or failure of a company's business model largely depends on how it interacts with the players within the industry and the competitive marketplace. Any business model can perform efficiently in a pure monopolistic or temporary monopolistic market conditions. As firms build technology and innovation-based products in isolation of market competition, they routinely deploy conventional business models. Moreover, many companies ignore the dynamic elements of business models and fail to realize that they can design business models to generate winner-takes-all effects similar to the network externalities that the high-tech companies such as Microsoft, eBay, and Facebook often create. A good business model creates sustainable cycles that, over time, result in competitive advantage (Casadesus-Masanell and Ricart 2011).

A transformative business model connects to new technology to meet the emerging market need within a given market ecosystem. Business models are usually referred as a routinized practice of delivering a bunch of interdependent actions with an objective of serving target customers in a given market environment. Therefore, attempts to introduce a new business models often fail. Business models are commonly reeled around recurring psychosocial, market-driven, and customer-centric features comprising the degree of personalization (versus standardization), a closed-loop process (against the trend of open loop arguments to support proliferation of products and services), co-creating assets, usage-based pricing, developing a collaborative ecosystem, and implementing business models through an agile and adaptive organization design (Kavadias et al. 2016).

The Helix Effect

The shift from conventional to new-generation organizational structure and business modeling can be broadly delineated as the helix effect in business. The core of the helix lies in disaggregating the traditional management hierarchy into two separate, parallel lines of accountability equal in power and authority but philosophically holding a new perspective. Successfully adopting the helix requires a transformational leadership, customer-centric business philosophy, and co-designing business models. The convergence of the shifts in management mindsets and a talent infrastructure lays the foundation of helix, which emerges out of entrepreneurship education and bottom-up business economy that many businesses do not currently possess (Smet et al. 2019). Most companies in the emerging markets are transforming their global value chains and planning to coevolve domestic firms with advanced economy multinational firms as a helix effect. Strategies like enhancing the capability and competence; investment in internal research and development; and globalization through strategic alliances, and mergers and acquisitions push local firms toward helix effect. These firms not only succeed in local markets over time but can also build global value chains. The helix effect is visible to the companies as vertical partnerships with large firms while horizontal collaborations with local network are jointly orchestrated (Saranga et al. 2019).

The helix in business is based on the concept of synergy that refers to the achievement through the sum of action across the business agents (elements of forward and backward linkages in various functions like innovation, manufacturing, supply chain, marketing, and value creation) within the system to catalyze the improved results than the individual efforts. Consequently, cooperation between these elements drives greater overall effect, as compared to the sum of the individual elements. These are joint effects, created by the collaboration between the agents of business helix. The convergence of demand-pull, technology, buying impulse, and value perceptions are emerging as major attributes to explain economic leverages of innovation in social and business ecosystems. The business model agents, therefore, have emerged as knowledge pool and a value-based asset in conceiving changing business propositions (Carayannis and Campbell 2009).

Commonly, two types of helix, double helix and triple helix, are observed in the business ecosystem. The coevolution of small firms with large business organization through strategic alliances on production, technology, distribution, or finance can be explained as double helix. Convergence of technology, entrepreneurship education, and public policies including the skill development programs, and financial incentive to promote small entrepreneurs are the active elements in the entrepreneurial helix process. Exploring new opportunities, right decision making in business, and developing a design-to-market strategy by building alliances with large companies have been the major focus of double helix approach of the small firms. In addition, firms also seek the patronage of large companies to lower the cost-risk ratio and augment profit. The success of double helix approach needs a transformational leadership at both business organizations to help in redesigning organization, creating value chain, developing global standards, investing in business process improvement, and strengthening the backward and forward business linkages.

Developing appropriate business models and infrastructure to implement business strategies, using contemporary technologies and user-generated information to support the diffusion of innovation, serves as co-created helix networks. In addition, good coordination of the divergent actions of public investment through corporate social responsibility is necessary to achieve the alignment of corporate objectives with the society. Consequently, operation with such agents of business model helps firms in increasing the adoption of innovations and constructing knowledge flows between different players in the business (Badillo et al., 2017). The coevolution of small and big companies enhance investment on innovation, technology, and research and development. Such mergers or acquisitions in the double helix approach help companies strengthen their marketing strategies by developing customer-centric branding and promotion strategies. The convergence of technology, entrepreneurship education, and public policies on entrepreneurship development programs promote hybridization, business performance, and corporate citizenship behavior ambidextrously between small and large firms. These factors are associated with the triple helix business-development concept.

The helix concept has been managed discretely in large firms as some lean toward serving the niche markets at the bottom-of-the-pyramid market segment. It is often challenging for the small companies to adapt to a structural business model over the traditional family-based organizational structure. Relatively larger companies also tend to replace complex matrix structures, and redesign the organizations and their decision-making processes. The cooperative strategy between competing firms, to nurture frugal or reverse innovations bring them mutual benefits, such as restructuring markets with co-created innovative products, acquiring knowledge and technological skills, the dissemination of creative business ideas. Such collaborative approaches enhance organizational efficiency toward exploring new market opportunities to create value among customers and ensure growth prospects in the competitive markets. Vertical cooperation in streamlined areas of business (markets, products or services portfolios, or technology) with clients facilitates the identification of opportunities and reduces product innovation-related risks (Tsai 2009).

The helix effect helps the firms move ahead quickly to exploit new market opportunities. In the helix process, the transformative leadership drives value creation and augments objectives, discusses business priorities, and improves performance against the goals and targets. The clear distinction of enterprise management and leadership helps in constructing the helix with agile structures (Smet et al. 2019). However, organizational and business transformations in small companies are more challenging as compared to the large corporations due to *command and culture* disintegration. Moreover, the complex nature of the transformational necessitates in an organization often increases its overhead costs and administration process. Therefore, firms prefer to operate through their established business route instead of following the change to explore new markets (Horn et al. 2010).

Double Helix

Small firms operating in niche markets often face the problems of conventional manufacturing process, obsolete technologies, capital limitation, and lack of updated knowledge. These attributes drive firms to compromise with the product quality and stay noncompetitive in the regional or global markets. Such business confinement needs small firms in emerging markets to coevolve with large firms and catch-up with them to improve the manufacturing and marketing processes, and improve productivity rather than engaging in frugal innovations for niche markets (Awate et al. 2015). Small firms in emerging economies often face the challenge to break the *glass ceiling* to explore market competitiveness with the frugal innovation strategies, and develop tactical marketing approaches to override close business rivals. Firms often fail in establishing the regional or global value chains and enhancing their business performance (McDermott and Corredoira 2010). However, Chinese small and medium firms have coevolved as local to global firms over time by establishing mutually beneficial arrangements. These positive outcomes demonstrate the double helix effect in business through carefully orchestrated market reforms. In a large industrial segment of automobile manufacturers of India, the double helix effect has been clearly visible. Many domestic auto-manufacturing companies including Tata Motors, Mahindra & Mahindra, TVS Group, and Bharat Forge have developed international strategic alliances with auto manufacturers and survived the transition in their business (Saranga et al. 2019). Most of these local auto-manufacturing companies have achieved market competitiveness in global markets. Broadly, China and India have survived the transition to open markets and have coevolved as big-emerging markets amidst the business space of many developing markets.

The business transformation process for firms appears to be a difficult proposition due to the limitation of resources and lack of leadership drive. As this process continues, business leaders, along with the public policy implementers, begin to approach global standards of manufacturing, marketing, and services. However, in any industry, there are a few laggards, who remain moored in the old ways, although most domestic firms tend to make some progress and exhibit new business opportunities (Kumaraswamy et al. 2012). These firms develop sophisticated backward and forward networks using technology-led supply and retailing operations. Transformation of business model of small companies include technology-driven customer services with focus on reducing the tangible and intangible cost to customer, provide convenience, lower conflicts, and disseminate effective communications (4Cs). The helix effect is an integration of business operations of small and large firms encompassing strategic alliances and processes improvements, and adapting to customer-centric management with a view to explore new markets and achieve competitiveness in existing marketing (Jonnalagedda and Saranga 2017). The forward helix concept indicates that the local companies with standardization aim to develop alliances with external companies to reach global markets. The reverse helix interprets the association of international companies with local firms to explore reverse innovations at a global scale. With the support of public policies and economic incentives to promote local firms in the emerging markets like China, India, and Brazil have upgraded their process technologies and manufacturing capabilities for developing alliances with large companies. The small firms adopt latest production and management technique to improve their business performance (Rajagopal 2021).

Triple Helix

Similar to double helix, the triangulated factors in business cause triple helix effect. The theory of triple helix postulates that the factors comprising entrepreneurship education, industry, and government are critical to converge technological skills, entrepreneurship education, and public policies to improve the business performance. The advanced management techniques moderate the triple helix to drive the business performance of small companies. In this helix, innovation and knowledge play a critical role to connect the local firms to a wider marketplace (Phillips 2014). The major attributes of business that cause helix effect are illustrated in Figure 5.1.

The major attributes of social and business ecosystem such as government policies, public–private partnership, and social governance

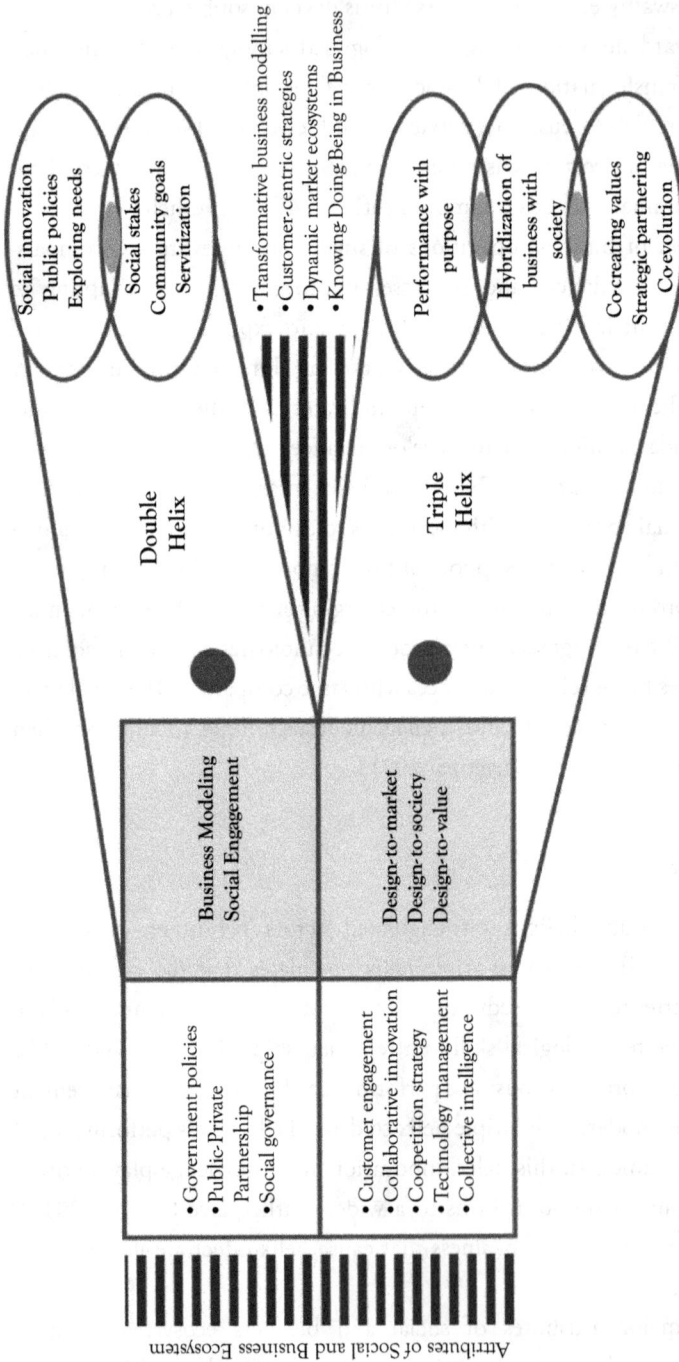

Figure 5.1 Helix effect and attributes of business

Source: Author.

contribute to the double helix process to moderate business modeling and social engagement as exhibited in Figure 5.1. The double helix stimulates co-crating social innovation, developing public policies, and toward exploring social needs. Firms also enhance social stakes, blend business strategies with the community goals, and in building servitization process as a result of double helix effect. Similarly, growing customer engagement, collaborative innovation, coopetition strategy, technology management, and mapping strategic and competitive views from the pool of collective intelligence moderate the triple helix (*e.g.* Etzkowitz 2003) . The business philosophies of design-to-market, design-to-society, and design-to-value constitute the triple helix, which stimulates firms to co-create performance with purpose, hybridization of social business and develop strategic partnership to co-create and coevolve customer values in business models. Consequently, most customer-centric companies are engaged in constructing transformative business modeling within dynamic market ecosystems by adapting to the knowing customers and society (knowing), implementing co-created business strategies (doing), and evolving as a value-based company (being) in the competitive marketplace.

Entrepreneurial education provides scope for exploring innovative ideas, which contribute in developing new markets and enhancing business performance. The technology space in the triple helix helps entrepreneurs and government institutions to draw relevant players from different organizational sizes, destinations, and various levels of business performance. The purpose of this helix is to formulate new strategies and ideas to achieve out-of-the-niche business performance. An innovation space emerges as the combined outcome of the triadic factors of triple helix (Kim and Lee 2016). The triple-helix system focuses on promoting innovation though homegrown (intermediate) technology, entrepreneurship education, and support of public policies. The triadic factors promote frugal innovations among the small firms, while this system has been most frequently used as a technological incubator. The triple-helix model and its indicators have been used to stimulate social innovations to improve the attributes of corporate citizenship and carry out the need-based corporate social responsibility (Cajaiba-Santana 2014).

The core of the helix lies in disaggregating the traditional management hierarchy into two separate, parallel lines of accountability—equal in power and authority but philosophically holding a new perspective. It is often challenging for the small companies to adapt to a structural business model over the traditional family-based organizational structure. Such business confinement needs small firms in emerging markets to coevolve with large firms and catch-up with them to improve the manufacturing and marketing processes, and the productivity rather than engaging in frugal innovations for niche markets. In the large industrial segment of automobile manufacturers of India, the double helix effect has been clearly visible. These firms develop sophisticated backward and forward networks using technology-led supply and retailing operations. The triangulated factors in business cause triple helix effect. The theory of triple helix postulates that factors comprising entrepreneurship education, industry, and government are critical to converge technological skills, entrepreneurship education, and public policies to improve the business performance (Phillips 2014).

Market Competition and Value Creation

Business expansion has observed a phenomenal change in the global marketplace over the years, which resulted into the economic dynamism in both developed and developing economies of the countries across the continents. Accordingly, many countries jumped into the market fray and started to produce a larger variety of products, making them more substitutable, raising the price elasticity of demand, and strengthening competition. Such market development had driven higher competition to modern growth and competitive firms aimed at larger territorial expansion at lower markups with prolonged break-even. As firms grow larger, they find it easier to cover the fixed cost on diffusion and adaptation of innovation and technology. As the size of the market is large with significant competitive driving force, the market innovation grows endogenously. This, in turn, pushes the market to grow exponentially, providing additional incentives to mount competition. The market economy thus moves in the global marketplace to the era of competition, which is consistent with the Darwinian theories of struggle for existence and survival of the fittest.

Market competition is inextricably linked to the consumer (human factors) ergonomics, perceived values, and user-centered consumption design. Cognitive ergonomics reflects the physical, cognitive and social needs, desire, satisfaction and values, quality of life perceptions, and goals of a person or team in the context of technology, environment, and culture, which enable consumers to associate with brands and companies in the marketplace (Lawler et al. 2011). Cognitive ergonomics focuses on the relationship of products and services with the cognitive capabilities of users. It draws on the knowledge of human perception, mental processing, and memory. Chaos among consumers causes unregulated flow of products carrying innovations with a disruptive edge. Such operational environment damages cognitive ergonomics of the consumers. Multinational companies are exploring consumer markets at the bottom-of-the-pyramid with a view to expand their businesses and explore new consumer experiences by widening mass-market operations in the low-end segments. These companies tend to achieve these goals through mergers and acquisitions of local companies, manufacturing using intermediate technology, and low-cost innovation. In the growing market competition, small firms always face major threat from large firms as the latter possess more resources such as physical infrastructure, finance, human resources, and technology. Most of the smaller firms, unable to continue their struggle for existence in the marketplace, develop cocooning attitude and confine to a niche. Often, large firms enter new market niches created by small firms through technological innovation and ingest the market share of small firms. Small firms are affected by entry of the firms that are similar in size and resources. Therefore, small firms play aggressive and defensive strategies to stay in the marketplace despite the competitive attacks by new entrants. However, consortium of small firms manufacturing identical products also poses major threat to large firm in sustaining the competitive marketplace.

In a growing market chaos among the several competitive products that have marginal differentiation, global organizations need to quickly develop the customer values to streamline the desired change in market and consumer attitudes. Large organizations if led well, can do more for more people and flip the chaos, complexity, and pressure to manage the new market endeavors. Niche marketing is often used as a deliberate marketing strategy to ensure business safety, increase customer value, and plan vertical expansion within the territorial limits. niche market players operate within a low-yield cycle and protect customer value. Various industries like consumer products and services, international technology, and business-to-business products are engaged in consortium manufacturing and marketing strategies to lower their cost of production and co-create products across destinations. The cooperative dairy industry in India and business-to-business products industries in China are the good examples of consortium business strategies. Therefore, smaller firms, through consortium, pose challenge to the large firms by adapting multiple market disruption strategies like low prices, disruptive innovation, mass marketing, and building customer loyalty at the bottom-of-the-pyramid segments (Rajagopal 2016).

Companies can take advantage of markets in such destinations and enjoy near monopoly for a short period as it takes time for the local competition to emerge. Companies can use this near-monopoly market situation to architect brand, set price levels, and deliver adequate customer value to generate brand loyalty. Most companies exploiting the latent demand realize the first-mover advantages and attain market leadership. The social and customer-centric innovations are converted over time into breakthrough innovations upon realizing its customer value and market behavior. Companies managing such innovative business projects reach beyond familiar domains and strive for divergent ideas, using widely crowdsourced and co-created ideas. To launch a successful breakthrough, companies need to consider the total number of inventions a company develops in a financial year for different markets, and the average performance of inventions in the markets in terms of market share and profit contribution of innovative products. The rate of success of breakthrough inventions can be measured through the customer values. The new product attractiveness may comprise product features including improved attributes, use of advance technology, innovativeness, extended product applications, brand augmentation, perceived use value, competitive advantages, corporate image, product advertisements, and sales and services policies associated therewith. All these features contribute in building sustainable customer values toward making buying decisions on the new products.

The Design Cube: Some Corporate Cases

Apple Inc:

Apple Inc. (Apple) has emerged in the global marketplace not only as a design company but also as a company engaged in co-creating customer value. The design perspectives of Apple enhance the scope of incremental innovation and concentric product innovations (vertical innovations across product portfolios). Though product designing is a centralized in-company process in Apple, it stays connected with the customers to understand their needs (expected solutions), emotions, and perceived values on the existing and new products of the company. Apple tends to develop empathy with the customers to gaining in-depth sense of customers' feel and emotions. Such customer-centric philosophy of the company successfully integrates the *design-to-market* (lead innovations, which are followed by the competitors) and *design-to-value* perceptive of the business model. Apple consider the voice-of-customers seriously, ensuring that it understands its users' needs better than any other manufacturer or similar company out there. The company follows the ACCA systems-thinking that emphasize the following attributes:

- Awareness (company to customer information dissemination)
- Comprehension (understanding customers and delivering then value)
- Conviction (developing products with user-centric technology and ergonomic designs), and
- Action (stimulating buying intentions by determining affordable price, augmented services, and anthropomorphic emotions).

Apple emphasized the core differentiator in its all products by understanding the customer needs and quick solutions. Pursuing the value canvas of customers, the company considered integrating all possible convenience in Apple products across the portfolios. Such product notion has boosted the *i-factor* effect in the market, which was embedded in all Apple products. For example, *iPhone* included communication, convenience, applications, leisure, and security factors, while *iPad* has been developed to support reading device, gaming and leisure, communication, and executive lifestyle). The Apple watch focused on designing this innovative product with powerful health and fitness applications, and as an ancillary communication device. Considering the design-to-market attributes, Apple watch has emerged more as a framework or series of products than a single product, whereas the earlier products of the company were launched with monolithic technological models.[1] This product enabled customers to monitor their physical health dynamics, support medical research, and helped them identify appropriate care for rising medical conditions. However, many customers did not perceive the need for smartwatches in general and Apple watch in particular as most functions used by the customers could be performed through the mobile phone (Bucic and Singh 2018). This attitude of customers has obstructed the company to manage the product with *design-to-value* approach effectively. Consequently, the asymmetric information between Apple and potential customers downplayed the behavioral attributes of customer to create value.

The societal values were upheld by Apple as the company moved into the school education (K–12 level) with the technology application for delivering educational programs including classroom and offline learning tools. Company has developed the classroom application to serve as a versatile teaching assistant that puts teachers in charge of every iPad and Mac in the classroom, so they can keep students on track. The Schoolwork application let teachers assign easily assign anything from worksheets to activities in educational apps, follow students' progress, and collaborate with them in real time. The company provides training to the teachers and students to use the application on either iPad or Mac computers. Apple has also designed augmented reality application for iPad to support easy and quick learning. The company has successfully established its values in the healthcare sector by providing the iPad and Mac users (patients and healthcare professionals) to work with health care application to monitor the social health scenarios. At home, iOS and iPadOS applications enable

---

[1] Monolithic design is a software development pattern in which an application is created with a single codebase, a single build system, and a single executable binary and multiple modules for business or technical features. Its components work together, and share the same memory space and resources.

patients to stay connected to their professional health care teams between office visits. Healthcare organizations also used CareKit, or off-the-shelf applications to create relevant applications that empower patients to manage their health. iPhone, Apple Watch, the Health app, and Health-Kit-enabled apps and medical devices make it easy for patients to record their health data and share it with their health care teams. These social care moves have added social value to the product-mix management strategies of Apple as it complied with the design-to-society attributes of the business within the *design-cube* architecture.

Apple is also able to generate social value by contributing to the sustainability. This is a carbon neutral company and by 2030 the company aims at complying with the international sustainability development goals. Apple follows the rules of circular economy and adheres to the sustainability commitments as it is engaged in developing innovative products from recycled materials and plans to work with the clean energy and no carbon footprint.

IKEA: *Integrating Social Values with Business Performance*

The Swedish furniture maker IKEA has slipped to the limelight of European market as a customer-centric company, which built its brand personality as a co-created design company by putting the customer first. The company aimed at coevolving with customers by transforming their ideas into innovative products and leading in the competitive marketplace by adopting the value-based business models. IKEA invested significant tine and cost to understand the customer needs, problems, solutions, and their values and lifestyle propositions to manufacture innovative products. However, this collaborative philosophy was undergoing a significant transformation in the recent past. Challenged by the rise of online shopping and changing consumer behavior, the company had to step out of their comfort zones and embrace new strategic initiatives to stay competitive. The company has identified customer value as value for money, and focuses on keeping the price low to make the products affordable to the customers. The work culture at IKEA significantly supports the objectives of frugal innovations, team culture, co-creation, and sustainability values, which helped the company grow along the social values.

IKEA designers work directly with woman artisans to develop the products in each collection, using traditional handicraft techniques, such as embroidery, weaving and pottery. The company co-creates unique products using traditional handicraft methods and materials, which results in limited edition collections, available at IKEA stores in selected countries and in the global marketplace.

The company is engaged in child development through creativity. IKEA had launched Play program, which is increasingly being recognized as the engine of optimal child development, future happiness, and achievement. Children today have less time for play, which hinders developmental opportunities as observed by the neuroscientists, social psychologists, and also business leaders. Therefore, IKEA moved into reconstructing perceptions of children by developing creativity, flexibility, resilience, and prosocial skills as essential attributes for survival and success. Most parents also recognize that playing has a vital role in helping children to be happy to express themselves and acquire creativity skills, semantic perceptions, and situational reasoning that will determine their ability to thrive later in life. Such social move of IKEA has crossed several value touchpoints between people and society, which contributed significantly to their business model by integrating the design cube in the following ways:

- Design-to-market (co-creation, customization, low prices, and high quality)
- Design-to-society (social values, social reconstruction, and social governance on development projects), and
- Design-to-value (customer engagement, ideation process, inculcating congruence of personal values with the company)

The structure of business organization in IKEA is informal and nonhierarchical, and it has team-based work culture engaging employees, stakeholders, and customers in managing creativity and market operations. The attributes of IKEA stores are simplicity, frugality, commitment, and value creation. The success of IKEA relied on efficient supply chain, creative designs, and operating on economies of scale to deliver quality furniture at affordable prices. The innate philosophy of the company was to run business with the *democratic design* policy comprising notions of, *for the customers* (manufacturing, marketing, and ensuring quality) and *by the customer* (customer engagement, experience sharing, creative participation, and value perceptions). The product design of each products considers five criteria comprising affordability, value for money, sustainability, customer preferences, and functionality. In order to develop effective customer engagement, IKEA teams work in closed proximity with the customers to act locally, which helps in minimizing material, packaging, and transportation cost (Alcacer et al. 2020). Such strategies of the company are converged with the design-to-society and design-to-value perspectives to maximize the effects of design-to-market strategies. Consequently, IKEA works with the creative business models, which meets the necessary requirements of the design cube concept.

The goals of IKEA to stay cost-effective and sustainable have helped company to acquire social values. Accordingly, the company has embedded the sustainability and circularity activities in the manufacturing of each innovative product. In 2002 IKEA introduced the IWAY standard for afforestation practices by getting all its wood supply chain from forests to furniture, which has created the new base standard of sourcing wood and planting new trees for every inch of wood used. IKEA group was one of the founding members of the Forest Stewardship Council, which aimed to fight against the deforestation practices of various wood-based industries. IKEA followed the principles of IWAY across countries as it has been the global procurer of wood (predominantly the company was sourcing timber from Russian forests). Such strategies of the company added high social values concerning sustainability and regenerating the ecosystem by adapting to the silviculture practices (Rangan et al. 2014). The social values have strengthened the design-to-society approaches of the company, which helped in gaining customer value and market competitiveness to the IKEA brand globally. While implementing the IWAY strategies and afforestation practices, the company found that managing forests has made IKEA a wood trader, which signifies to use the wood holistically and replenish within the biological cycle by planting a greater number of trees than the one that was felled for wood.

The vision of the company is to improve the lifestyle for the customers, coworkers, and the people who work at various supply sources. The vision further extends beyond home furnishing, to have a positive impact on the world through the communities, which creates the backward supplies links and a more sustainable life at home. IKEA aims at using more renewable and recycled materials; eliminate waste in manufacturing, operations, and marketing activities; and transform products and services through co-creation and coevolution. The two major raw materials for IKEA include cotton and wood used in manufacturing furniture, and the company ensures that these are sourced and used in a sustainable way to uphold the global concerns and social values. Since 2015, the company uses cotton from sustainable sources, which emphasizes that the cotton is either recycled, or grown with less water, chemical fertilizer, and pesticide, while increasing profit margins for farmers. In addition, the IWAY standard plays an important role in positive developments, ensures a safe and healthy work environment and at least minimum wages and overtime compensation, and prevents pollution to air, ground, and water. IKEA partners with the social enterprises, which include artisan shareholding companies, social enterprise foundations, and other companies addressing social challenges. Improving artisans' livelihoods is an important step toward helping them gain respect and create a better future for their families and communities, as an IWAY approach.

The company has more than 1,000 Indian women at the artisan collective *Rangsutra*, who are involved in the co-creation of beautiful, handcrafted textile products for IKEA. Similarly, collaboration with Doi Tung DP, Thailand, has so far resulted in several unique collections of handmade textile, pottery, and paper products. IKEA works with social entrepreneurs at both international and local destinations co-creating job opportunities. The company helps people who struggle to enter the labor market, for example, immigrant and refugee women. These attributes accurately fit into the design-to-society philosophy of the company. In another social value creation project, IKEA supported coffee farmers in the White Nile region of Uganda by collaborating with a social business project to buy coffee beans directly from about 13,000 small farmers. The collaboration makes it possible for them to have a steady income while learning more sustainable farming practices. Accordingly, IKEA contributed to better living conditions in the White Nile region through collaborative procurement, processing, and marketing the high-quality PÅTÅR, a special edition coffee, from Ugandan coffee growers.

The previous discussion on the IWAY, the vision, mission, work culture, and organizational structure of the company illustrates that IKEA complies with the fundamental attributes of the design cube integrating the three facets: design-to-market, design-to-society, and design-to-value.

Hindustan Unilever Limited: The Shakti Project of Women Empowerment

Project Shakti has been conceptualized by Hindustan Unilever Limited (HUL) to enable rural women in villages across India and cultivate an entrepreneurial mindset to make them financially independent. In an attempt to provide regular income, these women entrepreneurs (called *Shakti Ammas* meaning empowered women) are trained on basic principles of distribution management and familiarization with the company's products. A team of Rural Sales Promoters of the company coach, these women Shakti entrepreneurs by acquainting them with HUL products in order to manage their businesses better. This includes basic marketing approaches and troubleshooting solutions, and enhancing their soft skills on negotiation and communication. HUL had a long and value-based marketing practice in India (with market shares of nearly 60 percent) in categories such as soap, detergent, and shampoos, which has driven the value-based leadership of the company. HUL had decided to cover even the remotest market with its brands, and it had implemented an innovative approach to penetrate rural markets (with populations less than 1,000) with this strategic vision. Nearly two-thirds of India's population lives in this market segment, and the company had planned to empower rural women as HUL brand carriers within their neighborhood.

Shakti project was a win-win initiative taken by HUL to conquer the universe of market (premium, upper mass, economic mass, lower mass, and bottom-of-the-pyramid). The bottom-of-the market was aimed to be covered through the Shakti project. The broad task of the project was to promote sales and distribution of HUL products through several embedded initiatives as enumerated as follows:

- Communication initiative to build brands
- Micro-enterprise initiative to improve the livelihood quality and economy

- Social initiative to improve the social value and lifestyle
- Community initiative to bridge the socioeconomic inequality by augmenting income of women
- A business-diplomatic initiative to comply with the international voice on empowering women toward economic independence

Nonetheless, the concealed objective of this initiative for the HUL was to achieve scale of operation. The company's growth was within the close proximity of political developments. Despite the policy odds that emerged time and again, HUL aggressively sought the market leadership. The major challenge for the company was the growing unorganized market competition at the bottom-of-the pyramid (BOP) segment, wherein the low-price competition was looming manifold with the local players. With view to penetrate the BOP market against local low-price competitors, the Shakti project was launched in December 2000 in the erstwhile state of Andhra Pradesh in India. Its principal social objective was to provide sustainable livelihood opportunities for deprived rural women. Shakti entrepreneurs used to earn a small amount of distribution margin either by selling the HUL products to customers or local outlets. In this process, women entrepreneurs, as distributors, made 5 percent margin while the retailer had extended his profit typically to 8 percent. In the streamline initiative, the company offered Star Sellers an additional 2 percent premium to offset their selling expenses. To operate the sales and distribution tasks effectively, rural sales promoters were hired to coach women entrepreneurs and grow a viable business (Rangan and Rajan 2005). The first few months were the toughest and most entrepreneurs broke down to the cost-time-risk factors. Over time, the Shakti project had a new communication agent named as Shakti Vani (Powered Voice) to communicate with the customers and neighborhood people on health and hygiene matters.

The Shakti initiative of HUL is a perfect blend of performance with purpose by creating social values, corporate values, and market values simultaneously. This experiment was a good fit to the design cube concept as it explains all the three facets of the cube comprising design-to-market, design-to-society, and design-to-value. The business model of HUL is more social. This social marketing project has offered a silver lining in business to raise it to remote geo-demographics. This project benefited over one million rural women micro-entrepreneurs across 18 states in India. Project Shakti has helped to generate income by selling HUL brands to rural customers and has created a remarkable economic impact on the livelihoods of women.

Summary

Business modeling is practiced conventionally, but growing technology has driven multiagent modeling involving coopetition (cooperative competition), society, customers, stakeholders, collective intelligence, and public policies. An effective business modeling process entails not only the synergy among the business agents, but also the organization culture to implement the business model within various types of markets. The social value-based business models should define customers and their innate perceptions my mapping them on the storyboard and explain the underlying expectation of social and economic value rationale. Empowering stakeholders in customer-centric projects is a socio-psychological construct related to the individual's perception with the societal framework to live with the new business models. A business model is broadly considered as an interconnected and interdependent log of activities that determines the way the company portrays its role in the market along with customers, and key partners. Technology firms focus on creating innovative models and evaluating their efficacy. However, the success or failure of a company's business model depends largely on how it interacts with the players within the industry and the competitive marketplace. A transformative business model connects to new technology to meet the emerging market need within a given market ecosystem.

The theoretical framework of helix explains the effect of collaboration and synchronization with different factors on business modeling and innovation. The customer engagement to co-create research and development, innovations increases the scope of performance of firms in social and customer-centric innovations. The helix in business is based on the concept of synergy that refers to the achievement through the sum of action across the business agents within the system to catalyze improved results than the individual efforts. Developing appropriate business models and infrastructure to implement business strategies using contemporary technologies and user-generated information to support the diffusion of innovation serves as co-created helix networks. The helix concept has been managed discretely in large firms as some lean toward serving the niche markets at the bottom-of-the-pyramid market segment.

Helix effect is an integration of business operations of small and large firms encompassing strategic alliances and processes improvements, and adapting to customer-centric management with a view to explore new markets and achieve competitiveness in existing markets. The theory of triple helix postulates that the factors comprising entrepreneurship education, industry, and the government are critical to converge technological skills, entrepreneurship education, and public policies to improve the business performance. The triple-helix system focuses on promoting innovation though homegrown (intermediate) technology, entrepreneurship education, and support of public policies. The triadic factors promote frugal innovations among the small firms, while this system has been most frequently used as a technological incubator. In a growing market chaos among the several competitive products that have marginal differentiation, global organizations need to quickly develop the customer values to streamline the desired change in market and consumer attitudes. Various industries like consumer products and services, international technology, and business-to-business products are engaged in consortium manufacturing and marketing strategies to lower their cost of production and co-create products across destinations.

References

Alcacer, J., C.A. Montgomery, E. Billaud, and V. Dessain. 2020. *What IKEA Do We Want?* Cambridge, Harvard Business School Press.

Amit, R., and C. Zott. 2012. "Creating Value Through Business Model Innovation." *MIT Sloan Management Review* 53, no. 3, pp. 41–49.

Awate, S., M.M. Larsen, and R. Mudambi. 2015. "Accessing vs Sourcing Knowledge: A Comparative Study of R&D Internationalization Between Emerging and Advanced Economy Firms." *Journal of International Business Studies* 46, no. 1, pp. 63–86.

Bucic, T., and G. Singh. 2018. *Apple Watch: Managing innovation resistance.* London, ON, Canada: Ivey Business School.

Cajaiba-Santana, G. 2014. "Social Innovation: Moving the Field Forward. A Conceptual Framework." *Technology Forecasting and Social Change* 82, no. 1, pp. 42–51.

Carayannis, E.G., and D.F. Campbell. 2009. "'Mode 3' and 'Quadruple Helix': Toward a 21st Century Fractal Innovation Ecosystem." *International Journal of Technology Management* 46, nos. (3–4), pp. 201–234.

Casadesus-Masanell, R., and J.E. Ricart. 2011. "How to Design a Winning Business Model." *Harvard Business Review* 89, nos. (1–2), pp. 100–107.

Cash, J.I., M.J. Earl, and R. Morison. 2008. "Teaming Up to Crack Innovation and Enterprise Integration." *Harvard Business Review* 86, no. 10, pp. 90–99.

De Meyer, A. 2011. "Diving into the New Innovation Landscape." *IESE-Insight* 3rd Quarter, no. 10, pp. 21–29.

Etzkowitz, H. 2003. "Innovation in Innovation: The Triple Helix of University-Industry-Government Relations." *Social Science Information* 42, no. 3, pp. 293–337.

Horn, S.A., N. Forsans, and A.R. Cross. 2010. "The Strategies of Japanese Firms in Emerging Markets: The Case of the Automobile Industry in India." *Asian Business & Management* 9, no. 3, pp. 341–378.

Jonnalagedda, S., and H. Saranga. 2017. "Commonality Decisions When Designing for Multiple Markets." *European Journal of Operational Research* 258, no. 3, pp. 902–911.

Kavadias, S., K. Ladas, and C.H. Loch. 2016. "The Transformative Business Model." *Harvard Business Review* 94, no. 10, pp. 91–98.

Kim, J.Y., and M.J. Lee. 2016. "Living with Casinos: The Triple-Helix Approach, Innovative Solutions, and Big Data." *Technological Forecasting and Social Change* 110, no. 1, pp. 33–41.

Kumaraswamy, A., R. Mudambi, H. Saranga, and A. Tripathy. 2012. "Catch-up Strategies in the Indian Auto Components Industry: Domestic Firms' Responses to Market Liberalization. *Journal of International Business Studies* 43, no. 4, pp. 368–395.

Lawler, E.K., A. Hedge, and S. Pavlovic-Veselinovic. 2011. "Cognitive Ergonomics, Socio-Technical Systems, and the Impact of Healthcare Information Technologies." *International Journal of Industrial Ergonomics* 41, no. 4, pp. 336–344.

Magretta, J. 2002. "Why Business Models Matter." *Harvard Business Review* 80, no. 5, pp. 86–92.

McDonough, E.F., M. Zack, H.E. Lin, and I. Berdrow. 2008. "Integrating Innovation Style and Knowledge into Strategy." *MIT Sloan Management Review* 50, no. 1, pp. 53–58.

McDermott, G.A., and R.A. Corredoira. 2010. "Network Composition, Collaborative Ties, and Upgrading in Emerging-Market Firms: Lessons from the Argentine Auto Parts Sector." *Journal of International Business Studies* 41, no. 2, pp. 308–329.

Phillips, F. 2014. "Triple Helix and the Circle of Innovation." *Journal of Contemporary East Asia Studies* 13, no. 1, pp. 57–68.

Rajagopal. 2016. *Innovative Business Projects: Breaking Complexities, Building Performance (Vol.2)-Financials, New Insights, and Project Sustainability.* New York, NY: Business Expert Press.

Rajagopal. 2021. "Entrepreneurship, Education, and Economics: A Helix Effect on Business Growth." In *Entrepreneurship and Regional Development: Analyzing Growth Models in Emerging Markets,* eds. Rajagopal and Behl, R. New York, NY: Palgrave Macmillan.

Rangan, V.K., and R. Rajan. 2005. *Unilever in India: Hindustan Lever's Project Shakti--Marketing FMCG to the Rural Consumer.* Cambridge: Harvard Business School Press.

Rangan, V.K., M.W. Toffel, V. Dessain, and J. Lenhardt. 2014. *Sustainability at IKEA Group.* Cambridge: Harvard Business School Press.

Saranga, H., Schotter, and R. Mudambi. 2019. "The Double Helix Effect: Catch-up and Local-Foreign Co-Evolution in the Indian and Chinese Automotive Industries." *International Business Review* 28, no. 5, pp. 1–18.

Smet, A.D., S. Kleinman, and K. Weerda. 2019. *The Helix Organization.* New York, NY: McKinsey & Co.

Tsai, K.H. 2009. "Collaborative Networks and Product Innovation Performance: Toward a Contingency Perspective." *Research Policy* 38, no. 5, pp. 765–778.

Un, C.A., and K. Asakawa. 2015. "Types of R&D Collaborations and Process Innovation: The Benefit of Collaborating Upstream in the Knowledge Chain." *Journal of Product Innovation Management* 32 , no. 1, pp. 138–153.

About the Author

Rajagopal is Professor of Marketing at EGADE Business School of Monterrey Institute of Technology and Higher Education (ITESM), Mexico City Campus and Life Fellow of the Royal Society for Encouragement of Arts, Manufacture and Commerce, London. Dr. Rajagopal is Visiting Professor at Boston University, Boston, Massachusetts. He has been listed with biography in various international directories. He is serving also as Visiting Professor at University of Fraser Valley, British Columbia, Canada-India Campus.

He offers courses in the areas of marketing, innovation management, and international business to the students of undergraduate, graduate, and doctoral programs. He has imparted training to senior executives and has conducted over 70 management development programs to the corporate executives and international faculty. Throughout his career, Dr. Rajagopal has delivered a number of courses and executive and doctoral programs regarding the areas of marketing and international business in business schools including the Indian Institute of Management, at Indore and Rohtak, India; Narsee Monjee Institute of Management Studies, Mumbai; Institute of Public Enterprise, Hyderabad, India; and at International Management Institute, Bhubaneswar, India.

Rajagopal holds postgraduate and doctoral degrees in economics and marketing, respectively from Ravishankar University in India. He has to his credit 63 books on marketing and innovation management themes and over 400 research contributions that include published research papers in national and international refereed journals. He is Editor-in-Chief of the international journal *Leisure and Tourism Marketing* and the *Journal of Business Competition and Growth*. Dr. Rajagopal served as an associate editor of *Emerald Emerging Markets Case Studies* during the period 2012–2019. He is on the editorial board of various journals of international repute. His research contributions have been recognized by the National Council of Science and Technology (CONACyT), Government of Mexico, by awarding him the honor of the highest level of National Researcher-SNI Level-III. He has been awarded UK-Mexico Visiting Chair 2016–17 for collaborative research on "Global-Local Innovation Convergence" with the University of Sheffield, UK, instituted by the Consortium of Higher Education Institutes of Mexico and UK.

Index

OTHER TITLES IN THE MARKETING COLLECTION

Naresh Malhotra, Georgia Tech, Editor

- *Stand Out!* by Brian McGurk
- *The Coming Age of Robots* by George Pettinico and George R. Milne
- *Market Entropy* by Rajagopal
- *Decoding Customer Value at the Bottom of the Pyramid* by Ritu Srivastava
- *Qualitative Marketing Research* by Rajagopal
- *Social Media Marketing* by Alan Charlesworth
- *Employee Ambassadorship* by Michael W. Lowenstein
- *Critical Thinking for Marketers, Volume II* by David Dwight, David Soorholtz and Terry Grapentine
- *Relationship Marketing Re-Imagined* by Naresh Malhotra, Can Uslay and Ahmet Bayraktar
- *Service Excellence* by Ruth N. Bolton
- *Critical Thinking for Marketers, Volume I* by David Dwight, David Soorholtz and Terry Grapentine
- *Smart Marketing* by Ahmed Al Akber
- *Marketing Plan Templates for Enhancing Profits* by Elizabeth Rush Kruger
- *Launching New Products* by John C. Westman and Paul Sowyrda
- *Sales Promotion Decision Making* by Steve Ogden-Barnes, Stella Minahan and David

Announcing the Business Expert Press Digital Library

Concise e-books business students need for classroom and research

This book can also be purchased in an e-book collection by your library as

- a one-time purchase,
- that is owned forever,
- allows for simultaneous readers,
- has no restrictions on printing, and
- can be downloaded as PDFs from within the library community.

Our digital library collections are a great solution to beat the rising cost of textbooks. E-books can be loaded into their course management systems or onto students' e-book readers.
The **Business Expert Press** digital libraries are very affordable, with no obligation to buy in future years. For more information, please visit **www.businessexpertpress.com/librarians**. To set up a trial in the United States, please email **sales@businessexpertpress.com**.